for Jim
for Jim in the
wild country

Gary La Fontaine

Nov 20, 1999
Fullerton, CA

Fly Fishing
the Mountain Lakes

Summer of Discovery Series

Volume 1

Fly Fishing
the Mountain Lakes

by **Gary LaFontaine**

Greycliff Publishing Company
Helena, Montana

ILLUSTRATIONS BY Chad M. Peterson, Minneapolis, Minnesota

Charts on pages 20–21 are based on norms from *The Physical Fitness Specialist Manual*, the Cooper Institute for Aerobics Research, Dallas, Texas, revised 1998. Used with permission.

For information, address Greycliff Publishing Company, P.O. Box 1273, Helena, MT 59624-1273.

DESIGNED AND TYPESET IN CHELTENHAM CONDENSED
AND GIOVANNI BY Marcy Chovanak of Greycliff Publishing Company, Helena, Montana

COVER DESIGN BY Geoffrey Wyatt, Helena, Montana

COVER PHOTOGRAPH BY © Don Roberts, Lake Oswego, Oregon

10 09 08 07 06 05 04 03 02 01 00 99   10 9 8 7 6 5 4 3 2

LIBRARY OF CONGRESS CATALOGING-IN-PUBLICATION DATA

LaFontaine, Gary.
    Fly fishing the mountain lakes / by Gary LaFontaine.
      p.   cm. — (Summer of discovery series ; vol. 1)
    Includes bibliographical references and index.
    ISBN 0-9626663-7-8 (alk. paper)
    1. Fly fishing—Montana—Anecdotes. 2. LaFontaine, Gary.
I. Title. II. Series
SH317.L34 1998   98-28039
799.1'24'09786—dc21   CIP

DEDICATION

To James Sutherland

> As I get older I look up to the men and women who
> keep fishing well into old age.

He wrote to me:

> "I caught my first trout on a fly in 1933, and
> I assume that I will catch my last one on a fly,
> too. Although I am dragging 81 and pushing 82,
> I am still backpacking. Last Sunday I came out of
> the Middle Fork of the Stanislaus."

Ol' Jim Sutherland

In my experience I have seen a lot of old people, ranging in age from 15 to 90. Jim Sutherland remains young at 83.

CONTENTS

SUMMER OF DISCOVERY

Each summer season for me is a chance to learn and a chance to have fun. One without the other would make it a wasted summer. The books in this series are about the very good summers of my fly fishing life.

This first volume in the Summer of Discovery Series explores a special type of water. Share my educational and enjoyable summer fly fishing high-mountain and mountain-valley lakes. Mountain lakes have their own set of challenges, but there are lessons to be learned on other still waters that can be modified to meet the problems of fishing mountain lakes. The chapters in *Fly Fishing the Mountain Lakes* alternate between the goals of laughing and learning. The odd-numbered ones are about the fun of the summer. The even-numbered ones are the hard-core, how-to lessons. My original intention was to do a book of stories about my hiking and fly fishing days in the high country, but as I began to write, I realized that much of my enjoyment was linked to the discoveries I made. For me the learning and the fun are all one.

The how-to premise of this book is that a fly fisherman can't be a good mountain lake angler without being an all-around stillwater fanatic. Every great high-country fly fisherman of my acquaintance has two passions—stillwater fly fishing and backpacking. For the first they become experts on the richer, more complicated lowland lakes; and then take the techniques they need into the high country. The learning process for these fly fishermen, and for me, takes place on stillwater trout waters in my home area. For the backpacking, the young ones rely on strong backs, the older ones have had to get smarter.

Fly Fishing
the Mountain Lakes

CHAPTER 1

May 11th — *The first scramble for ice-out;*
a day at Ramshorn Lake

"NEVER DOUBT the courage of the French. We're the ones who discovered that snails were edible."

Bernie Samuelson looks at the escargot, watches me eat one, and stares again at the serving plate. At Chico Hot Springs they serve the best escargot in Montana, which is like serving the best prime rib in Paris; but I've had escargot all over the country and this is good. Bernie has to be as hungry as I am—simple meat-and-potatoes boy or not— and he will try one sooner or later.

He puts one in his mouth, chews carefully, and says, "Not bad."

"Sweet meat."

"I wonder if Rufus would like snails?"

After what that goat did for us, I would gladly buy Rufus a plate full of escargot.

BERNIE SAMUELSON and his pack goat, Rufus, are legendary among high-mountain lake specialists. For most of the summer he travels the state searching not just for fishing lakes but for fishing lakes at ice-out. When he goes high enough—up over 10,000 feet in the Beartooths—he can find ice remnants in late July.

There's something about legendary outdoor characters. They don't get their reputations by doing things the normal way. Simple fanaticism isn't quite enough. They do things that sane men marvel at but have no wish to emulate. They like to tell stories about the times they almost died—and if those stories aren't exaggerated too much, you're in the company of a legend.

Legends get nicknames. Jeremiah "Liver-Eating" Johnson? The man didn't get the nickname for table manners. Bernie Samuelson doesn't need a nickname because he has a goat. That's enough to tell him apart from all the other Bernie Samuelsons in the world.

After today I call my buddy, "Bernie 'the-goat's-the-smart-one' Samuelson."

BERNIE HITS more high-mountain lakes at or just after ice-out than any other person alive because he doesn't wait for the "sure thing," the "window of opportunity," or even the "long shot." I can't prove it for certain, but I'd bet that he has trekked up to some high lake after a few warm days in January just on the chance of a miracle thaw.

We drive to the end of the Buffalo Horn Road, already sliding through snow patches, and Bernie says, as we stand at the trail to Ramshorn, "There's a fifty-fifty chance the ice will be breaking up."

I let my two dogs out, Chester the Wonder-Mutt and Zeb the Rottweiler, and Bernie unlatches the trailer and leads Rufus out. Zeb looks at Rufus and doesn't know whether to mug him or mount him. The dog sticks his nose in the goat's face and Rufus licks his snout—they're friends for life.

We load up Rufus, settle into our backpacks, and start up the trail on a quick day trip to see if the ice is off. As soon as we start to climb we hit snow. Within a mile we stop and put on our snowshoes and the sprint to the top becomes a slog. I huff, my snowshoeing legs getting their first workout in years, and the dogs wallow in drifts. Rufus high-steps easily and Bernie smiles like a fool in paradise. I can't figure it out but soon I'm grinning, too, even though every muscle in my body is starting to break down.

"We just need a rim of open water around the edge," Bernie says. "A few feet."

Hours later we reach Ramshorn and it's frozen solid. A cautious man would drive a semitrailer across it without a second thought. Bernie jumps up and down on it just to be sure and the ice doesn't even quiver.

We build a small fire for a quick meal and sit there on a tarp, looking at the lake. Neither of us regrets the trip in. Anyone who can't understand this may be a fly fisherman, but they're not a high-mountain lake fly fisherman.

IT STARTS SNOWING and it is already nearly dark when we start down the mountain. The drifts seem deeper, harder to clamber over with the snowshoes, and impossible to break through. In the gloom of dusk and blowing snow only Rufus knows where the trail is; and with little tinkling bells he leads us out.

Chester, longer legged, keeps up, but Zeb bogs down in every deep drift. He watches me with a mixed look of fear and love—as if I'd ever think of leaving him—and I struggle back to pull him through. After the fourth time I fall flat in the snow. With a flashlight in his mouth, Bernie helps me rig a shoulder harness on Zeb, and we tie a rope from Zeb up to Rufus. The goat walks steadily until the rope tightens and then, as if he knows why he is doing it, he slowly edges ahead until Zeb pops free from the latest snow drift.

WE SIT in the restaurant at Chico, eating an appetizer of snails and drinking beer. A friend, Ron Ruddig, sees us and comes over. "How was Ramshorn?" he asks.

"Ron," Bernie replies, "We nearly died up there. We got hit with the worst spring blizzard I've seen in thirty years out here, the temperature dropped forty degrees, the wind howled, and it got dark hours before it should have."

"It's the word-for-word truth," I affirm.

"Rufus saved us," Bernie says.

Ron just nods, "Uh, huh."

"But I think that the ice might break up on Ramshorn next week," Bernie predicts.

And, a week later, I go back up there with him. The lake is still frozen solid.

CHAPTER 2

Ice-Out Strategies

HITTING THE PERFECT ice-out—the day everything breaks up—is one of those impossible dreams. Like winning the lottery. Obviously, someone wins, but it's never you. Or me. Well, actually it was me once. But short of camping on a lake for a month, there's no way to guarantee that you'll be there at the exact moment.

For one thing the breakup doesn't last even a day. The ice gets rotten, looking like a grungy Swiss cheese, and suddenly the wind shatters and disperses it. A large lake can clear in fifteen minutes. One minute maybe half the lake is

5

open water; minutes later the only ice left is chunks blown against the shore.

And when the ice disappears around the inlet stream at the head of the lake, it is the magic fly fishing moment. Not just when there's some open water. That's good— sometimes great—fly fishing, but it's not magic. Magic happens when any fool who can flip a fly fifteen feet catches the biggest trout in the lake, cast after cast.

It's not all luck. My friend Bernie Samuelson proves that. I asked him once how many times he's been on a lake exactly at ice-out. "Maybe two times a season, out of forty trips trying to hit it," he said. "Multiply two times ten years trekking the high country."

HERE'S THE ENTRY from my 1995 fishing log for my one perfect day (June 15th):

Dolus Lake:

Peter Giffen and I hiked up to check out lower Dolus. The purpose was as much to exercise the dogs as anything. For all we knew the lake might still be frozen. When we got there the lower half of it was open. No fish were rising, even though there were clouds of midges in the air, but this has always been a good lake for numbers of trout.

Zeb got a nickname. My Rottweiler puppy jumped from shore onto a floating slab of ice. As soon as he hit it the slab exploded under him. His paws slapped air with panicked paddling (the breed is not known for its swimming ability). "Icebreaker," Peter kept calling him.

Peter waded out to a boulder at the outlet, found back-casting room, and began retrieving a small nymph. He started hooking fish—8- to 13-inch rainbows and cutthroats—right away. He laughed, stopping only to admire each trout before letting it go.

Two hours later he left the open water to walk up and check out the inlet stream. I was no more than fifteen minutes behind him—as a matter of fact, I saw him stop at the inlet, look out over the ice, and keep going around the lake.

I was a hundred yards from the inlet when the wind came up the lake. The ice started hissing, a soft noise, and then it broke into small chunks. The current of the little inlet stream, Rock Creek, cleared out fifty yards of open water. Trout were rolling all over the surface—not jumping, but rolling.

I remembered what Bernie had told me, "If you ever hit breakup, use a streamer."

"Cutthroats aren't really fish eaters," I had replied.

"Just try it."

I waded through a bog to the mouth of the stream and threw out a size-10 Green Plain Jane. The fly didn't make it far—it never made it far. The first fish was a 16-inch cutthroat. The next ones were 14 inches, 20 inches (a rainbow), 17 inches, 15 inches, and 17 inches. There didn't seem to be a single small trout at the inlet.

Dolus is right above Deer Lodge, a fairly easy two and one-half mile hike and I've fished it five to ten times a year for almost twenty years. The trout in this lake run 10 to 12 inches on average. A 15-inch fish is a bragging specimen. I get maybe one or two that size a season. My best ever (before today) was 17 inches.

There I was, hollering and waving to get Peter to come back, and catching more big fish—big for this lake—than I ever thought existed here. I wondered how long it was going to last; and where these trout have been hiding all these years.

Then I realized that they haven't been hiding. They've just been spread out over a lot of water, mixed in with a lot of quick, eager small trout. Then, for a brief moment, they concentrate in one spot, apparently with no small ones around to compete for the fly.

BERNIE'S PREMATURE TRIPS to frozen lakes aren't even exploration. They're more acts of nervousness. He can't stand the anticipation (sort of like the way aquatic insects, not really ready to hatch, rise to the surface buoyed by internal gases).

For years he has kept detailed records of his treks to hundreds of lakes. He doesn't go into the mountains just to fish lakes. On every hike well into the summer he's trying to hit ice-out. Once he finds the first lake right at ice-out, he can predict when other lakes will break up. He is uncanny for the rest of the summer. He has the sequence for breakups charted: if Dolus Lake (in the Flint Creek Range) ices out on June 1, then Bass Lake (in the Bitterroot Range) will clear two weeks later. It doesn't matter if these lakes are in different mountain ranges, separated by hundreds of miles, because the same winter weather patterns usually affect the entire state of Montana.

Last summer I went on fourteen hikes with Bernie and his goat, Rufus—there were no trips to frozen lakes. We had wonderful high-mountain lake fishing twelve times. Bad spring weather knocked us out two times. We caught more fish in the early season than we did at midseason, but the real reason for hunting ice-out was that we caught big trout and grayling—trophy specimens—on every single lake.

During the early season Bernie only fishes lakes that have spring spawners—cutthroats, goldens, and rainbows. Also, he only hikes to lakes that have inlet streams. The inlet streams may be too small for actual spawning. They may even be temporary spring snowmelt. Bernie doesn't care. He just wants fish concentrated at an inlet.

THERE ARE THREE STAGES of ice-out:
1) Partial clearing—good to great fishing lasts a week or more;
2) Breakup—almost always happens in the afternoon; spectacular fishing (Bernie has never seen anything else); lasts a few hours;

3) Post-breakup—good to great fishing; lasts up to a month.

The easiest way to understand early season strategies is to study how fish act during each phase of ice-out.

THE PARTIALLY CLEARED LAKE

There are a lot of reasons one part of a lake thaws before the rest of it. Springs create open holes; internal lake currents weaken ice cover; a prevalent wind frees selected areas. Typically, the northwest corner of a lake gets the early season sun, but in rugged mountains heavy shade can mess up the natural progression of the melt.

Springs

Lakes formed in soft, fissured sedimentary rock, such as limestone or dolomite, usually have spring holes. Most high-mountain lakes, at least in Montana, don't have spring holes, because they are formed in areas with hard rock, basic igneous and metamorphic rock. There are exceptions. Two of my favorite spring-fed, high-mountain lakes are Rat Lake up Squaw Creek in the Gallatin River drainage (made famous by John Gierach in his classic, *A View from Rat Lake*), and Rainbow Lake up Gold Creek in the Clark Fork River drainage. Naturally, because they have springs, they are rich waters.

Springs are important at ice-out because trout try to spawn around them. The best approach for spring areas is one of the most basic stillwater techniques, the count-down method. Cast and let your fly sink, counting off the seconds. With each cast, keep counting longer and longer before you start retrieving, until your fly snags weeds, and then back up the count by one or two seconds. The best patterns include the Woolly Bugger, of course, but if there are springs with rich, alkaline water you'll find scuds, and a good scud imitation may be the most consistent fly.

How do you locate springs? Look for steam coming off the water on a frosty morning. Or look down in the water for areas that green up earlier and heavier than the rest of the lake.

Outlets

Natural Lakes, without dams, usually have a broad, shallow lip at the outlet. At ice-out these outlets fish better than outlets in man-made lakes. The shallow shelf, where the current picks up speed, provides good spawning habitat. On lakes with too small or blocked-up tributary inlets, the outlet is often the only spawning area. On lakes with good tributary inlets, the outlet shelf is second choice. It gets numbers of trout, but not the biggest ones.

It would seem that the best fly for spawners at the inlet would also be the best fly for spawners at the outlet. Nothing could be further than the truth. A streamer, the best fly at the inlet, is a lousy choice at the outlet—and this includes the generic Woolly Bugger. No pattern comes close to the dead-drifted egg imitation at the outlet.

It's easy to spot the spawning redds, lighter patches of gravel in the algae-rich outlet bottom, and with good light it's even easy to see the mating pairs of trout. The best casting angle is upstream, not across stream. Hang your egg pattern under a yarn or dry-fly indicator and let it drift drag free just off the bottom.

I've seen the egg work many times, including the trip to the Little Blackfoot detailed in this log entry:

> Steve Gayken and I stayed high on the bank, spotting and kibitzing, and Justin Baker covered the mating pair precisely. He put a Woolly Worm, Hare's Ear nymph, and

a scud imitation within inches of the male rainbow's nose, both with retrieves and dead drifts, and that fish never even nodded acknowledgement. Justin tied on an Orange Glo Bug and on the first drift the male bolted two feet ahead to grab it.

There's an obvious reason for the difference in response between the outlet fish and the inlet fish. At the outlet the trout are actually spawning, and while they're not actively feeding they'll still instinctively snatch eggs. At the inlet the trout are not spawning yet. They're staging to run up the creek. Not only are they feeding hungrily, they're aggressively fighting each other.

Ice Shelf

The ice shelf on a partially thawed lake, and how trout orient to it, fascinated me so much that we horse-packed scuba diving equipment into Hamby Lake, a 35-acre pond at 8,000 feet in the Big Hole drainage.

Bernie called me, "The ice is one-quarter off the lake, and with this nasty weather it won't clear for a week."

We rushed up the next day and prepared to answer two questions:

1) Are trout aware of a fly "crawling" towards the edge of the ice?

2) Are some areas of the shelf more productive than others?

Jenny Koenig did the scuba diving. Bernie was calling her the Blonde Ice Maiden until she splashed him. She submerged and the rest of us strung up fly rods. Bernie, Ken Mira, and I cast weighted Woolly Worms fifteen feet back onto the ice and dragged them steadily towards the water.

I hooked a 15-inch cutt-bow hybrid as soon as my fly plopped into the lake. It wasn't a surprise. It happens too often to be random luck. Jenny bobbed up in open water and confirmed it, "Your fish tracked that fly for the last five feet, and I'm not sure but I think he came up from the bottom when it hit the ice."

So question number one was answered—fish are aware of a fly moving towards the edge of the ice. To get their attention, use a heavy, large fly that makes an impression as it rasps across the ice. Even put a split shot or a second fly eighteen inches above the tail fly to increase the effect.

Jenny continued to swim along the rim of the ice, staying deep and moving slowly to keep from scaring fish. After twenty minutes she was chilled in spite of the heavy dry suit and extra insulation and came into shore. She told us, "Some trout cruise long stretches of the rim, moving back and forth. The best concentration of fish are where the ice edge is closest to the lake bottom, ten feet maximum. Over there," she pointed to a large curve of open water over the center bowl of the lake, "it's pretty barren."

So, the answer to question number two? Fish where the ice edge is over the shallowest water.

FISHING A LAKE BEFORE REAL BREAKUP

Both trout and grayling stay at the inlet mouth until the ice cover breaks up. They linger there for as little as a few days or as long as a month before migrating to their spawning sites. What determines when they go upstream? It's when the current running from the lake slackens.

Bernie and I camped for six days on Cliff Lake, a well-known big-fish water off the Madison River. We hoped to hit breakup. The rim of ice melted back a little bit each day, but we never got a warm and breezy afternoon that would have swept away the ice cover. We worked the outlet and along the ice shelf and caught nice cutthroats and rainbows steadily.

On the last day, when it was obvious we weren't going to hit breakup, Bernie said, "I'll show you a trick," and we pushed through slush piles up to the Antelope Creek inlet.

Bernie dropped a weighted bucktail into the rushing stream and stripped off thirty feet of line, letting the current take the fly under the ice. As soon as he began retrieving he hooked a large fish, so large that he couldn't pull it in against the current and he lost it.

Who says you can't ice fish with a fly rod? Anyone with any pride might have refused to catch trout like this. There wasn't anyone like that on this trip. We took turns, feeding the bucktail under the ice and hooking a fish on nearly every retrieve. Even with 3X leaders, we could only land the smaller ones.

FISHING A LAKE AFTER BREAKUP

Bernie's quest for ice-out on lakes in Montana goes from early May through early August—roughly ninety days. He's generally in the high country for sixty out of the ninety days. In that time he fishes about 10 percent partial clearing, 2 percent breakup, and 88 percent post-breakup conditions.

I don't push into the high country as early as Bernie does and my percentage of post-breakup days is probably around 98 percent. With the post-breakup period I begin the stalking and hatch-matching strategies. This is when I search not just for feeding fish, but for the largest fish feeding in a particular body of water.

High-mountain lakes aren't very complex environments. My stomach samplings put trout and grayling into one of three feeding groups during the post-breakup period:

1) Trout cruising and searching the surface for random food.

Forget them, after breakup these cruisers are almost always small trout. During the non-hatch periods there isn't much littering the surface, usually just a scattering of adult midges, and this isn't enough to get bigger fish searching the surface. The daily, predictable dumping of terrestrial insects onto the water won't start for nearly a month. In the post-breakup period terrestrials constitute roughly 20 percent of the trout's diet, and in the first few days after ice-out it's probably less.

2) Trout cruising and searching the bottom for food.

Trout and grayling cruise the littoral zone of the lake singly or in schools looking for active, exposed nymphs. This feeding activity occurs a lot during the post-break–up period because aquatic insects begin migrating from deeper water into the shallows as soon as the ice disappears.

The standard slog-and-flog technique will work—throw out a sinking fly, let it settle, and retrieve it, over and over again. But this blind casting is boring. It's not my game, and it doesn't have to be the game for any intelligent fly fisherman.

The movement of the fish isn't random. The swimming speed of either individual or schooling fish frequently correlates to the amount of available food in a particular lake. If there are weeds, and abundant nymphs, the fish move slowly. Most high-mountain lakes aren't like this—they have boulder or mud bottoms, and populations of larger aquatic insects are sparse. The fish move quickly, covering a lot of area.

My first experience with deep cruisers was in 1970 at Park Lake above Helena. My teacher for western fly fishing tactics, Dick Fryhover, took me out nearly every day that summer to a different spot; and this was my first experience with high-country stillwaters.

I stumbled onto a tactical discovery that day, one that has meant hundreds of additional trout and grayling for me from lakes over the years, and recorded it in my log book:

> Nobody was catching grayling, but standing on the rock, I was high enough to see the schools of twenty or thirty fish swim past. The problem was that they were swimming so deep and fast that by the time I saw them it was too late to cast to them.
>
> They seemed to be on a schedule. Every five minutes or so a school followed the same path. Whether it was the same school or not, I wasn't sure. I cast out a Montana Stone nymph and let it sink slowly six to eight feet, hoping to time it to the movement of the school. They came in so quick that I didn't have a chance to even start a retrieve. A grayling of about 13 inches, took the fly and the line tip jumped.
>
> I timed the next three passes better and even had enough warning to start a retrieve, but I never even had a hit. On my fifth cast I didn't retrieve (again) and wham! a grayling took the dead, sinking fly.

I kept playing with this all day and a slow retrieve outfished a quick retrieve 4 to 1 and no retrieve outfished a slow retrieve four to one.

In my fishing log I underlined that didn't three times—it was a lesson I wanted to remember. There are a few special retrieves I use in stillwaters, along with a few standard ones, but if anything I'm a specialist at not moving a fly—nymph, dry, wet, or streamer—on lakes.

The secret to catching cruisers is to see them and then time the pattern of their movement. Even if the surface is a little choppy, it's possible to spot fish if you are high enough. This means you at least need to stand on shore or on top of a rock to get a vantage point.

3) Trout feeding on emerging midges.

Once the ice goes out on lakes, most aquatic insects—caddisflies, mayflies, stoneflies, damselflies won't start hatching for at least a few weeks. This is just as true on valley lakes as it is on high-mountain lakes.

It's not so with midges. They are ready to pop out as soon as the first slit of open water appears on a lake. They must have some way of timing pupation—the last spurt of growth has to begin when the lake is still frozen over. The freshly emerged adults crawl out on the ice edges and the snowbanks.

Even trout in high-mountain lakes can get fussy about imitation when they feed on emerging midges day after day. My favorite flies, fished in tandem, are an Improved Buzz Ball and a Halo Midge Emerger. The Buzz Ball, matching a mating cluster of adults, provides visibility and functions as a strike indicator. The Halo Midge Emerger may range from size 14 to size 24, but it's always black—the early ice-out midges are always black on the lakes I fish.

I tie nine to twelve inches of monofilament into the eye of the Buzz Ball and dangle the Halo Midge Emerger off the back, greasing both flies with floatant. I cast into the middle of the rising fish and let the flies sit there. This can be nerve-racking when rolling trout are slopping like pigs at a trough, but even the slowest retrieve won't help and will probably hurt chances of a hookup.

Not all parts of a lake get the same number of emerging midges. The early season hatches are thickest in flat, shallow areas. Broad bays, especially if there is a dark bottom that warms in the sun, usually prove best. The outlet shelf, where the current gathers, and the silty, alluvial fan of the inlet often produce good hatches, also.

UNLIKE BERNIE SAMUELSON, most people don't have the time like to search and chart the ice-out succession of high-mountain lakes ever higher through the early season. Most don't even have the time to hike once or twice a week into the high country. For the backpacking angler, however, hitting these waters at or close to breakup is still the key to fabulous fly fishing.

There is a shortcut. I found the perfect one. I had a pilot fly me over the Bitterroot-Selway Wilderness Area last spring. He swung low over various lakes while I found names on a topographical map. In half an hour I knew if a dozen waters were still frozen, completely ice free, partially open, or even, from the look of the ice, about to break up.

You don't have to fly over an area yourself (although it's a nice luxury). You just have to talk to airplane and helicopter pilots who regularly cover an area. At one of our local hospitals there's a life-flight helicopter; and two of the regular people on the flights are fly fishermen. They gladly chart lakes for me. Out here the majority of people are fishermen, and all of them like to look at mountain waters.

CHAPTER 3

May 13th — *Getting in shape; how to know*

I CAN SEE the headline now: "Former So-So High School Athlete Grows Old, Gets Out of Shape, and Dies on First Hike of the Season."

A little bit wordy but it tells the sad story. During the winters I travel the country, speaking and teaching fly fishing classes. I love it, but late-night restaurant meals, irregular exercise, and a heavy travel schedule pack on extra pounds.

At this stage in my life it's time for me to get in shape and stay in shape. It's that or give up this love of fishing and hiking hard. I'm over fifty, but different people hit this fitness crisis at different ages.

MARCH STARTS with pain. Not excruciating pain. I've never been able to push myself that hard, but I'm on the climbing machine, stepping to the mantra, "Burn, baby, burn."

My first hike into a high-mountain lake won't be until late May or early June, depending on the spring weather, but I've made the mistake too many times of trying the first climb of the season out of shape. I suffered through it when I was younger; now such a mistake could prove fatal.

Training for high-country trekking is basically simple, but necessary for all but the super fit. A person has to work on two separate aspects of conditioning—aerobic capacity and specific muscle strength.

You increase your aerobic capacity by doing something that raises your heart rate. The "something" can be anything from square dancing to rope skipping. The American Heart Association recommends a minimum of twenty minutes of aerobic activity three days a week for cardiovascular health. But forget the minimum—pounding up a steep trail with a fifty-pound back has nothing to do with minimums.

During the winter I walk or climb stairs as much as possible when I'm on the road; and I do thirty minutes a day on a Nordic Track and jog outside if the weather is good when I'm at home. By April I'm running a few slow miles a day and by May I'm running and bicycling both.

Great aerobic fitness isn't enough. I know from experience. Every year friends come to Montana fit and trim, and then at the first steep hill their legs seize up. Walking or jogging on level ground isn't going to strengthen the specific muscles used in climbing.

The major climbing muscles, the vastus lateralis running up each thigh, could probably be conditioned most quickly

by a tailored weight-lifting program. My way is more general—
bicycling works this muscle area very well, and I do a lot of
that in the spring, but specifically I keep a stair-stepping
machine right by my front door and get on it every time I
go into or out of the house.

"Burn, baby, burn."

I'M IN SHAPE. Round's a shape, isn't it?

There's an easy way to judge fitness. Find a local quarter-
mile track and time a mile and a half run. That's six laps.
Match your time against this chart from the Cooper
Institute for Aerobics Research.

WOMEN	
THIRTIES	
below 13:44	Superior
13:44 to 15:20	Moderate
15:21 to 16:58	Minimal
16:59 and above	Unfit
FORTIES	
below 14:32	Superior
14:32 to 16:12	Moderate
16:13 to 17:29	Minimal
17:30 and above	Unfit
FIFTIES	
below 15:58	Superior
15:58 to 17:14	Moderate
17:15 to 18:31	Minimal
18:32 and above	Unfit
SIXTIES PLUS	
below 16:21	Superior
16:21 to 18:00	Moderate
18:01 to 19:02	Minimal
19:03 and above	Unfit

MEN	
THIRTIES	
below 10:48	Superior
10:48 to 12:38	Moderate
12:39 to 14:24	Minimal
14:25 and above	Unfit
FORTIES	
below 11:45	Superior
11:45 to 13:22	Moderate
13:23 to 15:26	Minimal
15:27 and above	Unfit
FIFTIES	
below 12:52	Superior
12:52 to 14:40	Moderate
14:41 to 16:23	Minimal
16:24 and above	Unfit
SIXTIES PLUS	
below 13:54	Superior
13:54 to 15:55	Moderate
15:56 to 17:32	Minimal
17:33 and above	Unfit

I TOED up to the line, my old stopwatch from high school track in hand, ready to smash that twelve minute and fifty-two second mark for the fifty- to sixty-year-old age group. I got a quick start, maybe too quick for a six-lap run—and at a half mile I was fourteen seconds ahead of pace. At a mile I was still six seconds ahead of pace.

But a roll of winter baby fat posed a problem. I could have handled the few extra pounds, but the weight just didn't keep rhythm with my fluid running style. Every time a leg went up, the belly bounced down, and vice versa. Up, down. Up, down.

By the last lap my legs were getting shorter. In running terms the "bear had jumped on my back." In scientific terms, my blood wasn't clearing the lactic acid quickly enough from my muscle cells. My fluid running form disappeared.

But I wasn't far off the pace with two hundred yards to go. I started my kick, knees lifting and arms churning. Breathing be damned—a heaving chest meant nothing. My sprint died only five feet from the finish, close enough for me to lean forward and keep staggering. I clicked the watch, but walked a full lap without looking at it.

Once around again, I glanced at the watch and shook it because you can't tell when these old watches will go bad. I scanned my magazine clipping again to make sure that the time for superior was twelve minutes and fifty-two seconds. I decided to have the track remeasured. I thought of finding a pay phone and calling the Cooper Institute to find out if they'd give me a handicap because of the 5,000-foot altitude.

I was close. Real close. Honest.

Note: The charts in this chapter are based on norms from *The Physical Fitness Specialist Manual*, The Cooper Institute for Aerobics Research, Dallas, Texas, revised 1998. Used with permission.

CHAPTER 4

Priming on the Valley Lakes

MY HOME REGION is sprinkled with incredibly rich ponds and lakes. Within an hour's drive from Deer Lodge there are two lakes and thirteen ponds that grow very large trout. They are great waters for fly fishing, shallow and weedy and full of insects and crustaceans.

For years these waters were an afterthought in my fishing, places I'd go to no more than a dozen times a season. My progression from casual to fanatic stillwater angler happened on these ponds and lakes, but it wasn't a gradual shift in focus. One day stillwaters were just an occasional,

23

slog-and-flog diversion—the next day they were the most exciting and challenging fisheries imaginable.

Everything changed on July 21, 1983. An English fly fisherman, James Harris, and I sat on the bank of the Hog Hole, one of the famous Anaconda Settling Ponds, and watched at least twenty men, some on shore and some in float tubes, beat the water all over the pond, the group hooking roughly one trout per hour. In British understatement, James said, "They're really very bad at this game, aren't they?"

James was not an unfair man. He would later write an article about the group of fly fishing friends who help me with scientific research, calling them "the greatest running-water fly fishermen" he'd seen in twenty years of international angling.

I didn't know the other anglers on the Hog Hole, but they fished the water pretty much the way I would fish it. They played slog-and-flog, throwing out a sunken fly—in most instances a Woolly Worm—and retrieving. The more sophisticated fishermen counted down the sinking fly, and worked it just over the weed beds. Most just threw a fly out and randomly pulled it in. These people, by the license plates on their vehicles in the parking lot, were from eight different states and one Canadian province. They were decked out in the newest equipment. They were probably a fair cross-section of North American fly fishing talent.

They were, in the words of James Harris, ". . . not very good at this game."

I knew what I disliked about pond and lake fishing—it was exactly this boringly random method of deep prospecting, even if it did produce an occasional trophy trout. Most of the anglers on the Hog Hole would probably be satisfied with one or two fish over five pounds, which was virtually guaranteed here with enough time on the water. None of us knew any better because, unlike the anglers of the United Kingdom, we weren't stillwater specialists.

James and I fished the Hog Hole for the next four hours. With him leading, and me following his example, we landed fourteen trout, the biggest an eight-pound brown. Those four hours changed my angling outlook forever. Over the rest of that season I fished stillwaters fifty-seven days, mostly in my home valley.

MY STILLWATER EDUCATION flourished into obsession, one that has never really died down, beginning that summer. Every new experience confirmed that stillwater fly fishing didn't have to be that repetitive slog-and-flog approach.

My education didn't progress evenly. It leaped ahead with bursts triggered by experimentation on local waters with a growing group of friends who were as fascinated as I was by our stillwater opportunities; my exploratory trips to hotbeds of North American stillwater fly fishing, especially the Kamloops region of British Columbia, to study the tactics of experts; and visits from English anglers steeped in their two-hundred-year-old stillwater tradition. It didn't take long for me to gather more than fifty distinct stillwater techniques, all of them effective, most of them relatively easy, and many of them visually thrilling.

Not all techniques worked on all stillwaters—thus the need for over fifty methods. My usual procedure, after arriving on the bank of a pond or a lake, was to climb a hill or cliff and just sit and watch the water for fifteen minutes before setting up any piece of tackle. The only exception to this observation period happened when trout were rising— and then I would try to start casting as quickly as possible. The trick when fish weren't rising was to guess which technique was perfect for that fishery at that moment.

TWENTY YEARS AGO it was hard for me to find anyone in my home area who even wanted to fish lakes. Now there's a bunch of us who hit the stillwaters in the valley regularly; with a quick telephone call I can get a few friends together for a trip.

My regular companions are Andy Stahl, Joel Hart, and Ken Mira. They live in the area and they actually prefer the ponds and lakes to moving water, fishing stillwaters a couple of times a week throughout the season. Another group, Bernie Samuelson, Matt Quinn, and Ron Ruddig, hit the lowland waters, but for them the valley ponds and lakes are only practice grounds until the mountain waters open up.

One evening in May, after a day on Georgetown Lake, we relaxed in an Anaconda restaurant. "On most of the high lakes I don't need all the techniques we use down here," Matt observed.

"But then there are other lakes where you wish you could carry in every bit of equipment you own," Ken rejoined.

"We can't," Matt answered. "That's the problem."

The whole group stayed there until closing time that night, playing with a problem of logistics. Which unique stillwater methods, honed on lowland reservoirs, were the most valuable in the mountains when the trout get difficult? Out of a bag of more than fifty techniques, which ones justified bringing extra equipment into the high country?

We eliminated some of our favorite methods that were effective on weedy, silt-bottomed valley lakes because they don't work well on the typically deep, rocky-bottomed mountain lakes. We rejected others because they require equipment, such as a boat, that couldn't be packed into the high country.

We discarded one method that stood at the top of everyone's list because it is so universal that it envelopes virtually every other technique. The most valuable technique in low-land lakes is spotting and casting to a particular fish; and this is also the most important trick on high-mountain lakes. But spotting, the skill that separates the beginning angler from the expert angler, is so universally applicable to fly fishing, in moving as well as stillwaters, that it is elevated to a level above technique. It is the umbrella under which every other method exists.

EVERY MEMBER of the group made a list of the ten "most unique and effective" methods for mountain lakes. Seven members and seven lists—there were three techniques that appeared on every list—three that everyone agreed are invaluable when trout in mountain lakes became difficult to catch. Two of the strategies were developed by someone in our group—a guarantee for the "unique" part of the qualifying standards—and the third, a United Kingdom technique, was a certain choice because it was the most exciting approach.

We even put these methods into their own categories: Most Exciting (Floss Blow Line), Most Effective (Hang-and-Bob), and Most Valuable (Multiple Roll).

Floss Blow Line

In the United States, stillwater anglers react to wind differently than do United Kingdom lake specialists. In the U.S. most fly fisherman will quit the water when the wind rises to anything more than a mild breeze. In England many anglers won't fish in a dead calm, even if trout are rising, but they'll rush to the water when it's blowing a gale and churning a lake to white froth.

That afternoon with James Harris at the Hog Hole a strong wind kicked up, sending spray into the air, and within an hour every angler on the pond rolled up his tackle and left. This left James and me with all the water, which was probably a good thing since we were going to use a method no one there had ever seen before.

I'd read about the Floss Blow Line, and had even thought of trying it. But I never acquired the right equipment, not bothering because I decided it was probably a limited technique that would only work in perfect dry fly situations. From what I had read, the method was an anachronism even on United Kingdom fisheries.

James strung up two long fly rods, each one more than 11 feet, and put reels on them filled with flat floss. Knotted at the end of each floss line was three feet of 4X leader material. The flies were palmered dry flies, a Soldier Palmer on his and an Orange Asher on mine.

The wind ripped the surface of the pond, peaking at twenty miles per hour. In this weather it was almost impossible to do anything other than dap a fly, but I had doubts about whether it was worth fishing at all.

James said, "It's easy," getting the wind at his back, lifting the rod straight up, and unfurling line. His fly bounced on the water a few seconds and then vanished in the swirling silver of a large rainbow trout.

Twenty anglers on the Hog Hole had caught seven fish in six hours that day. In four hours, the two of us landed fourteen trout—two cutthroats, six rainbows, and six browns—averaging more than four pounds in weight. Every fish came rolling or jumping at the bouncing fly.

The Blow Line Technique is no anachronism. It is an amazingly effective stillwater method in a heavy wind. My doubts about it were absolutely wrong. On mountain waters, where winds blow more often than not, it is almost an everyday strategy. While it's true that it is only useful in a perfect dry fly situation, strong winds on a pond or lake nearly always create that perfect dry fly situation.

It is one of the simplest fly fishing methods, but there are a few tricks to the technique:

- Get a fly rod longer than 11 feet and fill a reel with 90 feet of unwaxed floss (available in bulk rolls through a dentist).
- Use a light, hackled dry fly (a Bivisible is always a good choice).
- Position yourself with the wind at your back.
- Hold the rod straight up and feed 20 to 30 feet of line out into the wind.
- To touch the fly (or flies—it's possible to use two or three) on the surface, lower the rod slowly.
- Make the fly touch repeatedly in exactly the same spot. Don't let it skip randomly over the surface.
- Don't strike when a fish rolls on the fly. Do just the opposite—bow first, dropping the rod momentarily, and then strike. This movement will double the number of hook-ups.

It is important to pick the right area for the Blow Line method. The fly has to touch where the trout feed on top. The best spot in a strong wind is down wind from a point of land. No other place produces strikes more consistently with the Floss Blow Line. The wind pushes the surface layer of water, creating a current, and when that current hits a jutting piece of land it compresses and squeezes around the point. Trout concentrate behind the point to feed on the drowned insects swept along in the flow.

On the Hog Hole that day, James and I fished off the tips of the islands. Both ends of every island acted like a point of land, compressing current and collecting drifting insects. The trout positioned themselves like stream trout, letting the flowing water bring food to them.

Hang-and-Bob

The Hang-and-Bob matches up well with the Floss Blow Line. Neither method works without wind, but the Floss Blow Line is better in heavy wind and the Hang-and-Bob is better in light wind. The Blow Line, touching a fly repeatedly on the surface, is effective when trout are already feeding on adult insects. The Hang-and-Bob, a subsurface technique, is deadly when trout feed at a specific depth.

The Hang-and-Bob is a variation of the Right-Angle nymphing method used on streams. In Right-Angle nymphing a tuft of yarn, a bushy strike indicator, is tied at the end of the leader with an improved clinch knot. Another piece of monofilament, as short as six inches or as long as eight feet, is tied on right *above* the yarn indicator with an improved clinch knot. The yarn bobs along on top of the water and the piece of monofilament goes straight down into the water at a right angle and presents the fly to the fish. The big advantage of the method comes on the strike—there is no bend in the leader as it goes into the water to dampen the strike. When a fish sucks in the fly, the yarn is pulled straight down.

Our group wondered how the right-angle would work on lakes. Ron Ruddig was the first to try and he caught trout on Rainbow Lake. Bernie Samuelson had a fine morning with the hang-and-bob on Georgetown Lake. Andy Stahl became the biggest advocate for the Hang-and-Bob after a spectacular evening on the Hog Hole.

My first chance to try the method on a lake came at Clark Canyon Reservoir near Dillon. I paddled my kick boat to the mouth of the Red Rock River and set up with a breeze at my back. I cast straight downwind and settled in for some "bobber" fishing. I thought that this would be relaxing fishing, with the occasional trout, but the action was so steady that I had no chance to relax. Other fly fishermen on the water came over to look at the fly, but my success was from the method not the pattern. Everyone else retrieved nymphs, wet flies, or streamers, and no one was catching a lot of fish.

The Hang-and-Bob is bobber fishing with a fly rod:

- My preference is a light, soft action rod (8 foot, 9 inch for a 3-weight, weight-forward line) that protects the leader tippet on the strike.
- Tie on the main, six-foot, 4X leader and put a bushy piece of yarn at the end of this section; then tie a piece of 5X leader material above the yarn indicator.
- Use a nymph, wet fly or streamer pattern that is weighted toward the eye, so that with every up-and-down movement the imitation acts like a mini-jig. Bead-head patterns are ideal for this technique.
- Experiment with the depth of the fly, shortening or lengthening the right angle section of monofilament.
- Position yourself with the wind at your back.
- Cast downwind and let the "current " pull all of the slack out of the line.
- Keep the rod tip low to the water and watch the yarn indicator.
- When the yarn indicator goes down (it disappears quickly with a take), set the hook immediately.

The Hang-and-Bob works best in a light breeze. The yarn indicator rides the wavelets, bobbing up and down, and underwater the fly dances slowly up and down, too. The fly doesn't leave the area. It just keeps moving, a target that eventually teases even reluctant fish into striking. It's critical to not retrieve the fly. Any manipulation pulls the fly out of the area and ruins the effect.

The major challenge with this method is finding the right depth for the fly. Any imitation works best when it is moving at the eye level of the trout. My favorite variation with the Hang-and-Bob is to put two flies on the right-angle section of leader spaced about three feet apart. The distance between the patterns allows me to test two depths.

Multiple Roll

The most valuable fly fishing technique is the one that can bring a non-feeding trout rushing up from the depths to smack a fly. The only way to do that is to tickle a trout's curiosity, tease him to distraction, or even drive him into a competitive frenzy.

I happened upon the Multiple Roll by accident or, if my mediocre casting skills can't be called an accident, by fortuitous ineptitude. The method sprang to life, immediately complete, because my best roll cast flops out weakly instead of shooting out strongly.

I was hiking around the shore of Woods Lake, a trophy trout lake near Kalispell, casting as far as possible towards the middle. One friend, Gary Saindon, was also walking the bank and two others, John Randolph and Dan Abrams, were paddling a canoe. It was mid-afternoon in September, and although it was a rainy day, there apparently wasn't a single trout in the shallows. No fish broke the surface, and none cruised the littoral shelf that extended out thirty feet from the bank.

Wherever I had clear space for a back cast, I threw line far out into the lake, waited for a Red and Black Bristle Leech to sink deep, and retrieved the fly slowly into shore. A few, infrequent strikes happened just as the Leech reached the drop-off, the place where the shallows suddenly fell into the depths. The trout weren't feeding and they weren't in the shallows. They were holding in deep water against that steep drop-off wall.

I came to a section of bank lined with trees. There wasn't room for a regular cast. I had to roll cast the fly out beyond the drop-off. I made my first sloppy, big loop roll and the marabou Bristle Leech splatted about five feet short of the drop-off. I quickly made a second roll cast, shooting a few additional feet of line, and the fly hit right at the drop-off, still not far enough. I rushed a third and last roll cast, finally getting the fly out beyond the shallow zone. As it hit the water a rainbow slammed the fly.

I worked down the bank, using three or four roll casts to get the fly out, a necessary inconvenience as long as there were trees at my back. In less than a half hour, fishing a quarter mile of shoreline, I landed five more rainbows, all between two and four pounds. Obviously, the trout had shifted into a feeding mood.

Eventually I reached a section free of trees. I started making regular casts again, hauling and throwing a long, sweet line. I worked like this for a long time, never getting a strike, and I began to wonder about this. As my father used to say about me, "The boy's slow but when he gets hit on the head, he does rub the bump."

I felt silly using a roll cast with all that clear space behind me, but I started flipping the fly out with a three roll sequence before beginning the retrieve. Walking back over the water I'd flogged unsuccessfully with regular casts, I began catching trout again.

Gary Saindon, watching this, said, "There's no reason a roll cast should work better than a normal cast. Why should fish care how a fly gets there?"

For most of the fall I couldn't answer that question, but on a number of ponds and lakes the Multiple Roll Technique brought trout rushing to the fly during the slow times of the day. It became an important method for my friends in the valley, too. Joel Hart caught sixteen trout one morning on the Gold Creek Dredge Ponds and Bernie Samuelson, forced out of the high country by bad weather, camped on Georgetown Lake and caught extraordinarily big fish, averaging over two pounds, every day for two weeks.

My curiosity overwhelmed me. The answer couldn't wait until spring. I hastily arranged a scuba diving session, bringing in Brester Zahm to dive with me and setting up Joel and Bernie, the two people most familiar with the Multiple Roll, to do the actual fishing. We drove up to Woods Lake for two days of underwater observation.

We reached the lake when the trout were in a resting phase. The fish held against the drop-off, groups of them clustered on benches in depths from ten feet to eighteen feet. The first casts were normal—from the trout's point of view the fly landed and swam to the shallows, and even though fish turned toward the splat of the Bristle Leech every time, they lost interest as it moved over them.

The multiple roll casts produced a different reaction. The first cast landed short of the drop-off. The fly drew the trout's attention when it hit the water, but with the start of the second roll cast it accelerated and flew into the air. The trout were still looking at the spot when the fly hit again, five feet further out and right over their heads. The fish started rising up, three or four of them at a time, to look closer at this strange behavior, but the fly accelerated again and escaped just as they reached the surface. And then the fly hit the third time, behind them, and this time, in a mad race spurred by competition, one of them reached the Leech and slammed it as it began to swim.

From our underwater position, Brester and I watched Joel and Bernie catch five rainbows. Then we surfaced and made them change the method slightly. It was a small alteration, but it doubled the effectiveness of the Multiple Roll Technique. They still made the same first three casts—short of the drop-off, on top of the drop-off, beyond the drop-off. But then, instead of moving to a new spot if they didn't hook a fish, they kept roll casting, as many as five more times, just beyond the drop-off. The additional presentations gave any reluctant trout a chance to respond to the strange "fly away" creature.

The hardest part about the Multiple Roll Technique for a good roll caster is not casting too far the first time.

Here are my suggestions for equipment and technique:

- The best rod is powerful so that continuous roll casting doesn't tire you out.
- Use a floating weight-forward 7-weight line and a 5-foot leader tapered no finer than 3X (fish hit the fly hard).
- Use a streamer or a leech pattern—it shouldn't be heavily weighted.
- Stand on the shore and roll cast at least three times—just short of, right on, and beyond the drop-off.
- Repeat the last cast, beyond the drop-off, up to five times.
- If a trout strikes while you're actually roll casting, set the hook by hurrying the roll cast as fast as possible.

When fish are not feeding they rest in a safe place, usually under cover or in deep water at the drop-off zone. Resting fish, if they're not in a complete non-feeding funk, can usually be teased into chasing a fly.

The Multiple Roll Technique is one method that works even better in mountain lakes than it does in richer, lowland waters. The trout in high lakes are seldom so overfed that they ignore easy, or interesting, prey. The spoiled valley trout forget how to compete for food because they don't have to; whereas in high lakes the repetitive roll casts appeal to greed as well as curiosity.

THESE THREE METHODS, combined with a few more common techniques, form the core of a mountain lake strategy. The factor that usually determines the best method, at least when fish are in shallow water, is the wind. If the air is calm and trout are feeding, either a standard dry fly presentation for rising fish or a Spot-and-Cast presentation for deeper, cruising fish is a good tactic. In breezy conditions, with choppy water, the Hang-and-Bob is most effective. With a heavy wind the Floss Blow Line is not only easy to use when other methods are impossible but also deadly. The concept of wind management determines our approach when trout are shallow.

When fish move to deep water the wind is reduced to nothing but an annoyance—it no longer affects how and where trout feed in a lake. Our primary method in this situation is the Multiple Roll because it pulls fish to the top. If it doesn't work, then it's time to go deep with a searching technique such as the Count-Down Method.

Our group of stillwater fanatics use these methods all season, starting on valley lakes and ending on valley lakes. We don't just hit high-mountain fisheries during summer months. At times other fly fishermen join us for a day of fishing, but if they aren't stillwater specialists, they get lost in the animated conversations we have in the evening in a restaurant or a bar. To these people we might as well be talking about golf or tennis. That's how different stillwater fly fishing is from moving water fly fishing.

It's the work on the lowland ponds and lakes that can make you effective on mountain lakes. Develop an arsenal of methods, tackle, and patterns, focused on the challenges of mountain lakes, and fishing them with a fly will no longer simply be an afterthought.

CHAPTER 5

*June 1st — Going crazy; the World's
Smartest Fishing Dog (#1)*

MY BACKPACK has been filled for weeks. It sits in the enclosed porch, right by the door. It's there to tease, to build up anticipation; or sometimes as a taunt, useless in bad weather. I love the feel of it on my back and occasionally I have to put it on, adjusting the straps and shifting the weight until it's comfortable, and then I stand on my porch for a few minutes.

Some evenings, when I'm downcast about the long, cold spring, I put on my pack and circle the block. I stay on the sidewalk, going around two or three times, and I see my neighbors come to their windows and mouth words of pity, "It's just Gary with his backpack again."

The melancholy isn't over the lack of fishing, or even the lack of lake fishing—the season on low-elevation still-waters starts in March in my home valley. But mountain lakes don't mean just fishing. The words "fishing and hiking," or vice versa, are linked.

"Where are you going?"

"Hiking and fishing."

The sadness, after a long winter, is over the impossibility of even penetrating the high country, never mind fishing. Maybe, as a result of this lock-out, my friends fish the lowland ponds and lakes hard during the early season.

EVER SIT THERE, waiting for a telephone call, trying to do something, anything, to fill the day, when the only thing really worth doing was waiting for that call?

Mine finally came at seven one evening, and Andy Stahl blurted out, "I told you the old boy owed me. We're in. A week from Monday we can fish the pond."

Andy was so excited that he came over to my house the next morning to plot strategy. He wanted to talk about flies, tackle, techniques—everything had to be just right for this day of fishing. The "old boy" who owned the pond was a cranky son of a bitch, a retired army officer from the East who had bought his piece of Montana paradise and hadn't let any local people onto the best brown trout pond in the valley for nearly ten years. He may have owed Andy one day of fishing, but no way did he owe him two and, short of marrying the Major's ugly, divorced daughter, even Andy wasn't going to be able to get us in there again.

Andy talked until almost three in the afternoon and as he was opening the door to leave, he said, "And maybe you shouldn't bring Chester." Chester had been listening to our fish talk all day, getting more and more excited, and I swear that when Andy said this, Chester's face dropped and he looked for a moment like a basset hound that had been kicked. Then he slunk out the room.

"That was harsh."

"Nothing against Chester."

"Has he ever bothered your fishing?"

"You don't understand," Andy said. "It's not me. It's the owner. This guy makes fun of any dog that comes on the place. He thinks that he has the smartest dogs around."

"What does he do?"

"First thing he always does is sit his black labs down, put dog biscuits on the ground, and then he tells the dogs not to eat them. And the dogs won't until he tells them to."

"Chester goes with me."

"It's your call."

For the next few days I tied flies and trained Chester. No problem with that—teaching Chester wasn't like training, it was more a discussion about how things should be done. Chester quickly understood how he must respond to that biscuit laying on the floor at his feet.

Even before we climbed out of Andy's truck, the owner of the pond was crossing the yard trailed by two black Labs. The man scowled at Andy, as if he didn't remember him or the invitation to fish. When he spotted Chester he stopped suddenly, staring at my faithful mongrel like Chester might be a threat to his breeding bitches, and he asked, "What's that?"

I smiled, "That's the world's smartest dog."

The Major humphed, puffing up, and tossed a dog biscuit on the ground. "My dogs won't eat that biscuit until I tell them to."

Chester never moved and I said, "Neither will mine."

The Major glared, "All right. Let's see which dog will hold the longest."

That had me worried. I hadn't trained Chester for endurance, but there was no way to slip this contest. I told the Major, "You go ahead and set them."

He put his dogs in position, dropped a biscuit in front of each, and said, "Don't touch that." Then he walked over to Chester, dropped the biscuit, and in the same stern voice, meant to intimidate, said, "Don't touch that."

Chester, not easily intimidated, never dropped his gaze. He stared back at the Major for a moment; and then he looked over at the two Labs and, without a glance at his biscuit, trotted over, ate the other biscuits very slowly, and came back and sat in front of his.

"Damn," the Major said, more of a compliment than a curse.

And that's how we got in to fish the best brown trout pond in the valley, then and many times after. On occasion the Major would even call me and asked if I'd bring Chester out so he could show his friends, in his words, "The world's smartest fishing dog."

CHAPTER 6

From the Bottom of the Food Chain

ON SOME high-mountain lakes the food base can be maddeningly simple. The trout swim slowly and open-mouthed, like certain whales, straining minute, suspended food organisms known as zooplankton from the water. If zooplankton can grow something as large as a whale, why should a trout eat anything else? In many lakes the fish spend all summer and fall ingesting animals far smaller than a size-28 hook. Even if a fly fisherman could imitate individual organisms, it would be useless because the trout are not taking them one by one. The only "good" fly would

41

have a hundred incredibly tiny hooks dangling in the water, imitating a cloud of suspended zooplankton.

The zooplankton in high-mountain lakes is a predictable collection, including Copepods such as *Cyclops* and *Diaptomus*, Rotifers such as *Rotatoria*, and *Cladocera* (or Water Fleas) such as *Daphnia*. Most of these minute animals feed on algae, which means that populations will be at a peak when microscopic plants bloom in midsummer. That is when trout are most likely to feed on zooplankton exclusively.

The trout follow the zooplankton. Some of these planktonic animals have eyespots and, reacting to sunlight, they migrate daily. They reach maximum abundance near the surface early in the morning, but with growing illumination the animals begin sinking, reaching depths of fifty feet or more, depending on the clarity of the water, and stay deep until late afternoon. Then they begin a slow drift upward to the surface again.

THE NEED to understand zooplankton has little to do with imitation and everything to do with tracking the trout in lakes. If you find a shapeless, pastelike mass in the stomach of a fish, you have caught a plankton-eating trout. In clear lakes you should be able to spot these fish cruising slowly at a specific depth, but seeing them is different than hooking them. I logged a relevant experience fishing for plankton-feeders in 1996:

> August 7th through the 12th:
> Joel Hart is one of those fly fishermen who doesn't hike anywhere just to hike. He's in shape, and he'll walk miles to find an elk or deer during hunting season, but when he goes into the mountains to fish, he wants a sure thing. Four or five times a year he'll come with me to a

favorite high lake of mine; and two or three times a year we'll go to a favorite high lake of his.

But he refuses to take me to Cave Lake. "Never," he says, "Throw me in a briar patch. Anything, but not Cave Lake."

Joel is a stillwater specialist, one of the finest, and, like me, he loves a tough situation. Unlike me, he lacks a masochistic streak. He doesn't mind getting beaten by the trout, but he doesn't see why he should hike eight or nine miles uphill to do it.

He never should have told me about the goldens in Cave Lake—big cruising plankton-feeders. He shouldn't have telephoned me late one night, saying over and over, "I could see them, but I couldn't catch them."

STILLWATER SPECIALISTS in the United Kingdom learned how to catch plankton-feeding rainbows in their reservoirs, but at first they were baffled by the strange new trout in their country. Soon after Blagdon Reservoir was flooded in 1902, fishermen found that rainbows "disappeared" in midsummer. The normal surface- and shallow-water tactics didn't work for larger fish, especially during midday, on rich, algae-clouded Blagdon, or later on similarly fertile reservoirs such as Chew, Datchet, and Grafham. Anglers worked streamer patterns ("lures" in their terminology) on a full-sinking line. They anchored a boat in deep water and by methodically testing different depths they picked up trout on minnow imitations.

Peter Lapsley, in *Trout from Stillwaters*, explains the technique:

> The solution is to cast as long a line as possible, to let out line after the cast until we are sure that the lure is at the right depth and only then start our retrieve. Even a Hi-D line only sinks about one foot in three seconds and it takes a minute and a half to go down 30 feet. Count or

time as the line goes through the water. By doing this we should be able to return the lure to the same depth again and again with subsequent casts.

This method was specifically developed for the capture of rainbow trout, especially plankton-feeding ones. By mid- to late-June, the rainbows should have begun their assault on a rapidly growing plankton population. It would be quite impossible to represent daphnia or any other planktonic animal on a hook, and even if we could there would still be little chance of persuading the fish to select our artificial from amongst the vast host of naturals in the water. But, by some extraordinary stroke of good fortune, plankton-feeding rainbows are remarkably susceptible to bright, flashy lures. Gold, orange, yellow and red seem almost always to be the most effective colors, and a Whiskey Fly or a Dunkeld fished at the right depth and retrieved quickly will frequently provide the answer to an otherwise almost insoluble problem.

The pioneers of stillwater fly fishing in the United Kingdom perfected the Count-Down Method with sinking lines. It's a consistent technique for taking trout feeding deep on a variety of foods, not just zooplankton; and it's one of the keys for taking large trout in many western reservoirs in this country. The Count-Down and bright streamer patterns work on plankton-feeders in our lowland waters, too.

WHAT WORKED on United Kingdom reservoirs, however, does not work on our mountain lakes. The stripped streamer catches only the rare trout on high-elevation waters. There are too many differences—the cloudy, rich soup of the reservoirs versus the clear, sterile water of mountain lakes; an environment with numerous species of forage fish versus an environment with no bait fish except small trout (and not even those in lakes with no natural reproduction); reservoirs with rainbows and browns versus alpine fisheries with the much less piscivorous cutthroats and goldens.

Joel Hart verified the futility of streamers on the plankton-feeding golden trout of Cave Lake with four days of dog-crazy flogging, hundreds of casts producing not a single hit. Afterwards it was hard to convince him that these trout, the "strainers," are catchable. I had to work hard to persuade him to take me up to plankton-rich waters like Pear, Druckmiller, and Cave lakes.

> August 7 through 12 (continued):
>
> I've never seen anything like these lakes in the Crazies. We've been to three of them by now, sampling the zoo-plankton populations, and not only are the plankton populations high for a mountain lake, hundreds per liter of water, but they're also dominated by a single, bright red Copepod (*Diaptomus shoshone*). There's no doubt that trout in these lakes are concentrating on this particular zooplankton during the summer months. We kept two rainbows each from both Pear and Druckmiller for break-fast, and the flesh of these fish was a brilliant red.
>
> These fish aren't uncatchable—and after a great morn-ing on Druckmiller, even Joel is starting to have faith in that. We caught fourteen rainbows, the biggest ones over two pounds, but only one method worked. There may be more than one way to skin a cat, but if there's more than one way to skin these plankton-feeders, it's not in my bag of tricks. Maybe the "Hang-and-Bob" might be effective, but it would have to be with the right fly. The only thing that worked for us was "Pulling the Trigger" with the Rollover Scud.
>
> Joel kept saying, "We'll see if this catches those gold-ens on Cave."
>
> Of course the goldens on Cave are going to be the toughest trout to fool—among the plankton-feeders, goldens are always the hardest to catch. They lock so

thoroughly into a slow, open-mouthed swim-and-graze that they seldom even nod at a passing fly.

We moved over to the Sweet Grass Creek drainage and climbed to Cave Lake. We camped here three days and we could have pounded the water twelve hours a day in the long summer light. We didn't—we concentrated on the first few hours after sunrise and the last few hours before sunset. I did fish for a half hour during the middle of the day once just to see if the goldens could be caught then. By standing on a cliff we could see them, cruising with mouths agape, at least forty feet deep.

At dawn and dusk they were shallower, no more than fifteen feet deep, and with a Teeny T-400 sinking shooting head our flies would reach them quickly enough for the method to be effective. Just like the trout at Druckmiller, the goldens here looked at an Olive Rollover Scud, but took an Orange or a Red Rollover Scud much more aggressively. How aggressively depended on the flip or roll of the fly in relation to the fish.

Nothing makes a trout react faster than a Rollover Scud *if* the fly flips over close enough to the fish. The pattern swims upright when it's retrieved, but it rolls over as soon as the tension is gone. Or the movement can be just the opposite—it will sink upside down, but as soon as the angler tightens the line the fly will spin into the upright position. Either way it has a built-in "action" that triggers an instinctive response in trout—even prompting a reaction from the plankton-sucking goldens of Cave Lake.

Joel and I took turns sighting for each other. When the fly was at the correct depth—among, next to, or in front of the trout—the spotter gave the call. The angler pulled on the sinking pattern and the fly rolled quickly upright; and then immediately the fishermen slacked off and the fly flipped upside down again. Then he tugged sharply. With this multiple flipping movement we each caught a number of the goldens on the Rollover Scud.

Morning of the 9th—3 trout   Evening of the 9th—1 trout
Morning of the 10th—7 trout   Evening of the 10th—3 trout
Morning of the 11th—6 trout   Midday on the 11th—1 trout
Evening of the 11th—3 trout

Our tally for three days was twenty-four of the "uncatchable" trout. The morning was always better than the evening because fish were in shallow water longer. We caught the one midday golden to prove that plankton-feeders could be hooked in very deep water. The T-400 head, sinking at eight inches per second, took more than a minute to reach the proper depth. Working a fly at forty feet isn't something I'd ever do regularly, but there are anglers who fish very deep water and I can only admire their patience. The smallest trout were 12 inches, but many of the fish were 16 to 19 inches. We saw some cruising goldens that looked even bigger.

Joel couldn't believe that we finally caught the goldens of Cave Lake. This was the greatest trip for goldens for either of us.

The Rollover Scud flips because it has a strip of heavy wire lashed to the top of the hook shank. This weight unbalances the fly. The rollover, an action we started playing with to catch the overfed trout of the limestone ponds and spring creeks of the Deer Lodge valley, doesn't depend on the trout's hunger to elicit a reaction.

The Rollover Scud triggers an instinctive, snatch-it reflex in trout when it's fished right. The best retrieve, known as Pulling the Trigger, is a "pull slowly, stop, pull quickly" sequence. Let the fly sink to the eye-level depth of the trout. To move the Scud nearer, draw line with a smooth, slow pull, until the pattern is within two feet of the fish. Then stop retrieving, letting the fly flip over and sink. Finally, if the trout hasn't already taken it, tug sharply on the line to make the fly turn upright and jump forward a few inches.

A CONVENTIONAL FLY usually fails on golden trout—the Rollover Scud doesn't. A twist on the theories of imitation explains why plankton-feeding fish, oblivious to any regular food organism, respond at all to a certain class of "action" flies. A regular pattern depends on its visual characteristics to mimic life, and this is fine if the fish is feeding on something that can be imitated visually. The problem is that visual characteristics appeal to the urge to feed, leaving the trout a choice. For any fish grazing on zooplankton the choice is easy. He is going to ignore a conventional fly, no matter how lifelike it looks, and continue swimming open-mouthed through the cloud of minute food organisms.

A fly that moves suddenly and strangely, especially if it's close, works on a deeper, more reflexive part of the brain. It doesn't mimic any single prey item—with motion it mimics not just "life" but odd and vulnerable life. It somehow jolts even a grazing fish out of its stupor and excites it into eating a larger pattern. When the trout sees the strange, quick movement of the active fly, it has no choice, at least not about making that first instinctive move toward the pattern.

The closer the Rollover Scud is to a trout when the fly flips, the higher the chance of a take. This is why sight-fishing with the pattern is so effective. The angler knows when the fly is in the striking zone. On some waters the Rollover Scud can be four or five feet away from the fish. When it turns over, a cruising trout will rush to take the fly.

The goldens on Cave Lake weren't nearly that responsive. If the fly was within two feet when it flipped, a fish would turn to it and maybe take it. At this range he was more likely to keep swimming towards an Orange or Red Rollover Scud than an Olive Rollover Scud. If the fly was within one foot or, even better, six inches, when it flipped, the fish would almost always suck in the pattern.

Chapter 7

June 24th — Getting in; finally in top shape

I LOVE to hike almost as much as I love to fish. The truth is that, at least in Montana, you don't have to walk far for great fishing. There are plenty of rivers and lakes just off the road. But tramping far isn't a negative for anyone who loves the high country; it's a bonus for the fit.

> June 24th (log entry):
> Today's the day I hit the target time. Breaking the twelve minute fifty-two second barrier for the mile-and-a-half run made me feel good. There were bragging rights

there: "Well, yes, I am a superior specimen for the fifty- to sixty-year-old age group."

I don't know who that's going to impress, but it's probably not worth pitching to anyone under thirty.

Some people are in such superb shape that they can grab a heavy pack and just climb steep trails. They don't need specific conditioning to get ready for high-altitude walking. And they are usually young. As tempting as it may be, try not to hate them.

I was like that once. So were my buddies—it was nothing for Jay Gaudreau, Larry Dunnigan, Kevin Priard, and me to throw together eighty-pound packs and crush miles of mountain trail. And if we wanted to take in more than the packs would carry, we would grab grocery bags full of food and carry one each in our arms all the way. On flat sections we would jog the path.

Now my buddies and I are smarter—we have to be. If we weren't, we probably would hate the young and the strong.

June 24th (log entry, continued):

We parked the car at the Berry Lake trailhead and Kevin Priard said to his son, "Go ahead, Brent, let the dogs out," and Brent, more than ready, bounced around back to uncage the animals.

Kevin rearranged Brent's pack and, when he was finished, lifted it onto the young man's back. He started up the hill ahead of us. We didn't even try to catch up, but after a few miles Brent stopped yelling down to us, "You old boys still alive?"

The heavy pack he was carrying began wearing on him, and with our steadier pace we drew even with him at the five-mile point. He was too proud to whine, being a 21-year-old college football player, but he wasn't talking much anymore, just grunting and shifting under the weight.

We reached the flat, rocky ridge overlooking the water together. There was not even a breeze, up top or down below, and we could see big cutthroats rising on the lake. Nevertheless, we sat down to catch our breath and let the sweat dry in the sun. Not even Brent argued over the stop.

That's when Kevin asked, "Who wants a cold beer?"

Brent's head jerked around, "You brought beer up here?"

"No," Kevin said, reaching over and peeling back a zipper, and taking a six-pack from Brent's pack.

High-country invaders range from the purist, someone carrying everything on his own back, to the barbarian, bouncing along on a thunderous ATV. During any given fishing season my own trips hit both extremes, leaning more toward the pure end.

But I'll be damned if I'm going to walk up some boulder-humped road when I can ride an ATV and get to the fishing hours quicker. That's my choice on a favorite cluster of small lakes above Deer Lodge. I can base at the Rattlesnake Creek Campground, living out of my Volkswagen van, and reach Abicaulis, Alpine, Big Pozega, and Dead lakes in twenty minutes. The road is too rough for even the best-equipped four-wheel-drive truck, but it's easy with an ATV. The walk, which never feels right to me because it's on a road, takes four hours in and two and a half hours out on gravel and rock.

RATHER THAN HATING the young, you can just rent one. That's what Randall Kaufmann does on his August hikes with Joe Burke into the Wind River high country. He hires a young bull. His "Sherpa," he calls him. Randall carries a thirty-five-pound pack and the stud muffin lugs a ninety-pound pack.

June 24th (log entry, continued):

Those beers tasted so good we drank two apiece; and Brent was glad to get rid of the weight. The trout down below kept rising and we just sat up there on the ridge. This was dumb. I knew it was dumb because the first rule of high-mountain lake fishing is that when the trout are rising, drop everything and fish, because you don't know how long the rise is going to last.

We should have raced down that mountain. But we didn't. After almost an hour we strolled down to the lake. By the time we got to the campsite the afternoon clouds were boiling over the ridges and raindrops were starting to fall. We pitched the tents before everything got wet, and by the time we were finished the big fish were done feeding on the surface.

For three days, through wind, rain, and occasional patches of sun, we watched the water and never saw another rise. We didn't have float tubes or kick boats, and even if we could have reached the best places we didn't have the tackle we needed for deep-water techniques. We worked the shoreline with floating fly lines and near-surface tactics for hours each day, dog-crazy flogging, and, between us, we only caught four fish. All I could think about was the hour when trout were in close, cruising and sipping, and we sat on the ridge.

And every time I drank a beer it tasted bitter. We could have snuck reel spools and fly boxes into Brent's pack instead.

THE ANSWER IS, "A goat."

Is backpacking the main reason, and fly fishing only an afterthought, for going into the high country? For some it is. My definition of "getting in" may be different from a person who focuses on the hiking. Usually, I'm not satisfied just getting into a mountain lake. I want to have all the fishing equipment I need to catch trout. I can carry a fifty-pound backpack, but on a multiday hike that means counting ounces and making choices. The weight limitations are too restrictive on tackle even for an unproductive, uncomplicated mountain fishery. And it's impossible to carry all the rods, reels, lines, and flies someone might need on a rich, varied water.

Forget for a moment the rods, reels, lines, and flies. There's another piece of equipment, one of the most important for stillwater fly fishing, and packing it very far is impossible. A flotation device—for me it has to be an inflatable kick boat, not a float tube—gives the fly fisherman access to all the areas of a lake that the crowds don't fish. A stretch of shore with a cliff, a bay surrounded by a bog, or an overgrown slope are protected from the land-bound angler.

The high lakes in Montana, even those ten or more miles from the trailhead, get plenty of visitors during the summer months. It's almost a tradition on these waters for campers to eat a few trout for a meal. On the accessible side of the lake the fish are smaller on average, by as much as two or three inches. A kick boat, which has enough room for Chester to ride on the back, is the simplest secret for success on stillwaters. But my Tote-and-Float weighs twenty-six pounds, and the neoprene waders, wading boots, and flippers weigh another five pounds. That's too much additional luggage for me to carry. So, the question is, "What's the best way to take in everything you need?"

I'VE NEVER HIRED a "Sherpa," but I've worked with every other kind of pack animal. In order of preference, from worst to best, they are: horse, mule, llama, alpaca, and goat. I don't ride any of them, but they can all carry camping and fishing gear.

Horses

If you're just backpacking, and you meet horses coming the opposite way, step off the trail at least ten feet on the downhill side, not the uphill side. Don't talk loudly, move quickly, or look the horses in the eyes. Hold on to any dogs.

That's about as close as I want to get to horses in the back country. My brother Jay and I use his horses, Nick and Mountain Ash, and they're more trouble than they're worth. One person has to spend all his time taking care of them on a back country trip.

Horses have a sense of humor, but being rather dumb animals, they lean toward the most basic kind of slapstick. We walk, leading the horses, and when we stop Nick always takes an extra step forward and puts a metal-shod hoof right on top of my foot. No other horse ever does this so consistently, so it can't be coincidence. He looks at me like I'm crazy while I scream and shove to get him off, and he just shifts more of his eight hundred pounds onto the leg pinning me to the spot. He rears his head high, so I can't smack him, and with his fluttering eyelids and flapping lips, he laughs.

I know how to ride a horse. I also know that almost anyone who has ridden a lot has broken something at least once—and this probably happened on flat ground. Getting thrown and breaking something in the back country, far from medical help, would be an even grimmer experience. If it can happen to an experienced rider, it's far too likely to happen to the proverbial dude.

Ralph Cutter describes a situation in *Sierra Trout Guide*, "It's a real hassle attempting to get good photos from a horse; it's usually worth the effort to dismount. I had one moron get thrown from his horse when he used a flash bulb."

Mules

Mules are smarter than horses, but they don't have a sense of humor. They can be stubborn and nasty. It takes someone who really knows the animals as individuals to handle a string of them. They're more sure-footed than horses, not nearly as likely to hurt themselves, but they still have no compunction about hurting you. A mean one will do it on purpose. They also require a lot of tending and care in the back country.

Llamas

Llamas spit. They're closely related to camels. They're incredibly sure-footed on the trail, easy on the land as they graze, and pretty mellow around the camp. They won't kill themselves or you, but they can't carry anywhere near the weight that a horse or mule can carry (roughly 80 pounds versus 150 pounds). They're also very expensive. When a string of llamas and a string of horses meet on the trail, the horses get real skittish.

Alpacas

Alpacas are a smaller relative of the llama, but they're sweet, affectionate animals. They cost a lot, but the hair is valuable and selling it helps defray the expense of keeping one. They can't carry as much weight as a llama—roughly 40 pounds—but they're just as sure-footed.

I admit that I'm prejudiced. Ken Mira and his alpaca, Cheesecake, pack with us all the time and that animal is just plain lovable. She's easy to walk with and she's calm around camp. She's still a "herd animal," however, and she has to be tended as much as a horse, mule, or llama.

Goats

Just about everyone who packs with a goat has a story of the animal saving his life. John Mionczynski (author of *The*

Pack Goat) tells about the time his goat suddenly stopped and wouldn't go any further, and a few seconds later an avalanche of snow smothered the trail ahead of them. Matt Quinn was clambering down a rock slope to reach a stream and tumbled thirty feet. As he lay there, half-conscious and with a shattered ankle, wondering if he could survive a cold night, his goat climbed down and lay down next to him and kept him warm. Bernie Samuelson was confronted by a large male cougar, and as he stood with no weapon at hand, his goat Rufus charged past him, nearly disemboweled the cat with a sweep of his horns, and ran him off.

All of these behaviors are natural for a goat. He's intelligent enough not to get himself killed; he bonds closely with his owner and will usually lay down next to him or her (laying his head in a lap); the dominant male in a group protects the does and kids, this instinct so strong that he will sacrifice his own life. No one has ever told me about any other pack animal purposely saving his life.

The difference with a goat is that if it is raised by a person, preferably bottle fed and kept close to its owner, it doesn't think like a "herd animal." It becomes a true pet, not just a beast of burden. A horse always thinks it's a horse; a llama always thinks it's a llama, but a goat thinks it's a person. The psychology is much closer to that of a pack society—a wolf pack—than it is to a herd mentality.

No one has to lead a well-trained goat with a rope. He follows his owner everywhere, up and down trails, around the camp, and along the stream or lake while the person fishes and ignores him. He doesn't need much attention, but he does enjoy being talked to and even seems to listen. He can go anywhere faster and more sure-footed than a human, and he feeds on such a wide variety of plants that he does less damage to the land than any other kind of grazing animal. A big neutered male, called a wether, weighs over 200 pounds and can pack 60 pounds fifteen miles a day.

Just think about everything you can carry with that 60 pounds—drink, food, camping gear, fishing equipment, and a flotation device. This is not the purest way of going into the mountains, but my days of holy denial are over. They went with my youth.

I want a goat.

June 29th (log entry, back into Berry Lake):

[Berry Lake, in the Big Hole River drainage up Pioneer Creek Trail, is only eleven acres and would be susceptible to over fishing, but it's so remote that the cutthroats live long and grow big in the surprisingly fertile pothole. From Skytop Lake to Berry Lake there's not much of a trail. You must pick your way along the Divide; and only a goat could pack this stretch.]

We didn't walk this time; we packed up the goats and we trotted at a steady pace. The whole trip up took two and a half hours. Bernie Samuelson had his goat Rufus, Matt Quinn had his goat Rufus, and Butch August had his goat Rufus. All three Rufae come from the same breeder, a man who names all the males Rufus and all the females Matilda. All three are neutered males, long-legged Alpine/LaMancha crosses bred specifically for packing. The goats carried all the camp gear, food items, and four kick boats, and I carried a full array of fishing equipment.

The piece of equipment I thought I'd need least, and tossed in as an afterthought, ended up being the most important one on the trip. I took up a reel spool of floss blow line for dapping, but Berry, with a deep center bowl, isn't great dapping water. The best places for dapping are shallower, weedy stillwaters, where insects burst out and skitter all over on a windy day. On some high-mountain lakes, where the trout concentrate along the shallow shelf, dapping is not as efficient as casting to individual risers.

Today was the exception because a big cloud of deep water, egg-laying blood midge adults were spread all over Berry. They were the largest red midges I've ever seen, nearly a size 18, and the gusting wind was bouncing them along the surface all the way across the lake. I saw the slashing rises, which should have been a giveaway, and still guessed wrong—I get so used to midges on still-waters that I just assume that most of the trout have to be feeding on the emerging pupa. Bernie, Matt, and Butch, three of the most dedicated high-lake specialists around, also started with pupa imitations and did poorly, too.

I strung up the floss blowline on the 11-foot 3-inch loch-style rod and pawed through the piles of fly boxes for a suitable dry fly. Thanks to the Rufus boys I had all of my stillwater flies and finally found what I was looking for, a size-18 Orange Bivisible, and I tied it on and mer-rily launched myself and Chester out onto Berry. I picked out an area where trout were working, waited for one to show himself, and let the little Bivisible tap the surface once, twice, three times. It's those controlled, multiple touches on the water that make the fish come rushing to grab the imitation. In four hours I caught one cutthroat after another, fish up to three and a half pounds, and all of them took the dancing fly with wild, slashing strikes. But I wasn't alone—I had the only dapping outfit, so the other three guys anchored in a line next to me and we took turns hooking trout, passing my rod up and down the line.

We celebrated with a dinner of pork chops, fresh corn, and wine—thanks to the Rufus gang because I don't carry bags full of groceries in my arms anymore. The goats strolled around the campsite, the little bells tinkling in the dark, and the dogs, six of them among the four of us, waited for scraps. All of them waited except Zeb, who was tied up to a tree because Rottweilers don't beg, they demand.

Berry Lake was such a discovery that Bernie Samuelson and I went up there four more times during the summer. We packed all the tackle we could on Rufus because it is a tricky fishery. It is one of the few high-mountain lakes that requires deep-nymphing techniques—lead lines at twenty to thirty feet with the slowest possible retrieve of a Red Variegated Midge Larva. And when the trout do rise they concentrate in specific areas of the lake and feed selectively on the prevailing insect. The serious angler needs a flotation device and a full range of tackle and flies for this bit of paradise.

The best high-mountain lakes all present unique problems. For me, getting to the lake means getting there with enough fishing equipment to solve the toughest problems. That's the reason I fish. I'll ride in a four-wheel-drive truck or perch on an ATV; if I have to I'll sit on or pack a horse, when the distance is too great and the weight too much; but my favorite way to get into the mountains is by hiking. I've gotten spoiled over the last few years by my three friends and their pack goats. The animals make it easy, carrying extra equipment and a few luxuries. This is something I would have laughed at thirty years ago, but my pride as the purest of backpackers disappeared with my youth and the help is something that I surely appreciate now. It helps me see a future, thirty years or even more, where I'm still humping it into the high-mountain lakes.

CHAPTER 8

Equipment for Stillwater Tactics

MY DOG, Chester, rode on the back of my kick boat. My brother Jay was in an identical kick boat, an inflated blue oval with a hole in the middle, and the two of us used fins and oars to race across the lake. We started casting against the cliffs of the far shore and soon Jay hooked a fat, 13-inch cutthroat. My faithful dog seemed a bit upset as he watched Jay play the fish, but he stayed firmly planted on my kick boat. It was a touching display of his confidence in me. I didn't get a strike on my first few casts, but Jay soon hooked another nice cutthroat. My boy Chester stood up and paced a bit on the back platform of the kick boat, but then he sat down and stared at me. It was a touching display of his devotion to the one who cared for and loved him. My next few casts were ignored by the fish, but Jay quickly hooked a third big cutthroat. I heard a splash and turned around to see Chester swimming over to my brother's kick boat. It was a disgusting display of a "catch-fish-or-cut-bait" mentality that grips overly competitive fishing dogs.

With the kick boats that day on Big Creek Lake we caught trout that ran between 12 and 15 inches. There were plenty of other people camping on the lake, even though it was a steep, eleven-mile climb from the trailhead to the lake, but not a single one of them had a flotation device to reach the far shore. A troop of thirty-two boy scouts, a horse packer with six clients, and twenty-one other backpackers were all fishing and keeping trout for a camp meal, but the cutthroats they were catching along the accessible shoreline only ran between 8 and 11 inches.

On any trip into the high country, even with pack animals lugging part of the load, every ounce of equipment has to be justified. An inflatable kick boat, in its carrying case and with fins, boots, waders, and life vest, weighs close to thirty pounds. I've taken that load many times on goats, alpacas, llamas, and horses, sacrificing some food or camping gear. In desperation I've also thrown the kick boat on top of my regular pack—which itself weighs fifty pounds for a weekend trip—and beat myself to death carrying in a lake-crossing craft. If I can't take a kick boat, a special, lightweight backpacker's float tube, weighing about ten pounds with fins, waders, boots, and life vest, goes with my gear.

I CAN'T TELL SOMEONE what they *must* bring into the high country. My backpacking friends, all stillwater experts have different preferences than I do; and with each of them the equipment fits his or her grab bag of tactics. My equipment lets me cover a lake my way.

The actual brand names of tackle are included for reference. My listings are not meant as recommendations. The products are my actual fishing tackle, and these items work for me. I haven't done extensive comparisons between various brands, and there are surely products as good from other manufacturers.

What follows is an extensive list of specialized stillwater equipment. The beginner at lake fly fishing probably isn't going to purchase the full array immediately. The first rod to own is one that many running water anglers already have—a long (eight feet or longer) 3-, 4-, or 5-weight rod. That rod, with a floating line and a sink-tip line, is enough to catch trout feeding on the surface or in the shallows.

Rods

The best rods for hiking the mountains are not the multi-piece pack rods. This has nothing to do with the design qualities of the rods—it has everything to do with walking. Of the three rods in my high-country gear, one is a four-piece breakdown model and two are two-piece models in old aluminum rod cases. Those long rod cases serve as walking sticks, especially on steep trails where the arm muscles can help the leg muscles on uphills and downhills. Here's what I use:

- 9-foot 6-inch, 8-weight two-piece (Scott Eclipse)
  This heavy rod is mostly for deep presentations with sinking lines.

- 8-foot 9-inch, 3-weight two-piece (Sage LL)
  This is my basic dry-fly and shallow-water nymphing rod. The soft tip of the rod protects the fine tippets used

with small midge imitations. The light line lands softer than a heavier line and doesn't spook trout as badly in calm conditions.

- 12-foot, 7-weight four-piece (Winston LT Spey)

    This rod has two purposes. It's for dapping in the wind with a floss blow line—an important technique for me—and it's for bank casting. Most of my lake fishing is from a kick boat, but there are times when it's too much trouble to put on waders, boots, and fins and go out in the kick boat. For those brief periods the long rod is great for casting from the shore. When trees are tight to the water's edge, with no room for a backcast, you can easily roll cast sixty feet of line.

Reel

- STH #2 IM Cassette

    My one reel for mountain lakes is the kind with plastic cassettes. These quick-change cassettes, nine of them, are filled with different types of fly lines. This reel also has a smooth drag system, important for protecting fine leader tippets.

Lines

The greatest difference between my stream fishing equipment and my lake fishing equipment is the number of fly lines in my arsenal. For stream fishing there are two types of lines, a floating line for dry flies, shallow-water nymphs, and small wet flies or streamers, and a slinky rig, which really isn't a fly line at all but a monofilament running line with a slime line coating (Dai Riki Shooting Line), for bottom-dredging nymph fishing. I use floating line 98 percent of the time. For lake fishing I carry nine lines and, while the floating line is still my mainstay—the choice for roughly 70 percent of my stillwater fishing—I use the other lines a lot during a season.

- Floating line—full, weight-forward line with a dull, olive finish for the 8-foot 9-inch, 3-weight rod (Teeny Professional Series)

  On calm days trout in lakes, with no current riffling the surface, spook easy. A fly line, more than anything, shouldn't hurt my chances of catching these fish. It has to be light, a 3-weight dropping more softly than an 8-weight on the water. It has to be a dark, not light, and it has to have a dull finish, not a shiny one. It has to be a weight-forward because sometimes on stillwaters distance casting is important.

- Floating line—shooting head for the 9-foot 6-inch, 8-weight rod (Scientific Angler Ultra 3 Shooting Taper Floating Line)

  Sometimes distance casting is really important, especially when fishing from the bank. This is not a dull, dark-colored line (there are no dark shooting tapers in a floating line on the market). It gets dipped in green Rit dye. To hide the splash of the heavier line I make the leader at least sixteen feet long.

- Floating line—full-length, special-taper weight-forward with a mist green finish for the 12-foot, 7-weight rod (Scientific Angler Mastery Steelhead Floating Line)

  I carry this full-length line with its long rear taper for smoother roll casting, for the long rod. This rod and line combination allows for those sixty-foot roll casts.

- Floss blow line—90 feet for the 12-foot, 7-weight rod (no brand—it's just dental floss)

  This is flat, unwaxed dental floss, wound on a plastic cassette, for blow line dapping. The floss is available in bulk rolls from a dentist.

- Sink-tip line—weight-forward, pale fluorescent yellow line with a 15-foot, dark brown sinking-tip section for the 9-foot 6-inch, 8-weight rod (Orvis Hy-Flote Sink Tip Line)

Slow retrieves with a nymph often inspire subtle takes by the fish. With a regular sinking line even the most intent angler will miss these strikes. With a sink-tip line the juncture between the floating and sinking sections acts as a strike indicator, signaling the slightest tug on the fly. I use a sink tip for slow retrieves and a full sinking line for moderate and fast retrieves.

- Sink-tip line—weight forward, yellow line with a 5-foot sinking mini-tip for the 8-foot 9-inch, 3-weight rod (Teeny Mini-Tip)

  Jim Teeny put on a lake fishing presentation in a large, glass-sided tank at a sportsmen's show. He demonstrated how different sinking lines act in the water. As he cast the mini-tip line, he said, "I love to spot fish cruising along the bottom, and this is the line that I use to get a fly in front of them quickly. The 'quickly' is the important thing."

  The mini-tip is the perfect line for presenting a nymph in six feet or less of water. It doesn't plummet right to the bottom, pulling the fly below the fish, like a full-sinking line. It's better than a floating line and a long leader because it gets a fly near the bottom faster.

  The problem with deep cruising trout is that they are hard to spot until they get close. With a sink rate of three to five inches per second on the mini-tip, you don't need much time to get a fly near the bottom. You can control the exact depth of the presentation by changing the weight on the fly or the length of the leader.

- Intermediate line—weight forward, neutral density, amber line for the 8-foot 9-inch, 3-weight rod (Orvis 82-foot Intermediate Line)

  This neutral density line is only slightly heavier than water. It sinks just under the choppy, wind-driven current

on a lake. It stays straight during a retrieve, instead of belly-
ing, and this allows much better hook setting with a shallow, subsurface fly.

- Full sinking line—weight forward, black line for the 9-
  foot 6-inch, 8-weight rod (Scientific Angler Uniform
  Sink V with a sink rate of six inches per second or, as an
  alternative, the Teeny T-400 shooting head with a faster
  sink rate of eight inches per second)
  The modern lines sink uniformly. The tips are a slightly
  higher density than the belly, eliminating sag in the line
  for better, direct-pull hooking. These are the lines I use
  for the countdown method. When the bottom has large
  rocks or sunken trees that eat flies, carefully counting
  down before retrieving is the only reliable way to skim
  the fly over fish-holding structure.

- Lead core—30-foot, shooting-head, green line for the 9-
  foot 6-inch, 8-weight rod (Cortland 450-grain
  Kerboom)
  For me this line is not for plumbing the deepest waters
  imaginable with a fly rod. It's possible to catch trout in
  thirty to fifty feet of water, and sometimes—especially
  when goldens are sucking minute organisms—it's tempting to fish those depths, but the fly rod is not an efficient
  tool for deep presentation. I limit my bottom fishing to
  depths of ten to fifteen feet (depending on my boredom
  threshold that day).
  The lead-core line is for a special technique called the
  Yo-Yo Retrieve that is indispensable on valley lakes, and
  only occasionally useful on mountain lakes. The reason
  for this disparity is that rich valley lakes have soft, mucky,
  weed-covered bottoms and, with a few exceptions, mountain lakes have open, weedless bottoms. The Yo-Yo
  Retrieve works on rich, high-country stillwaters that are
  formed in soft earth instead of scraped out of rock. With
  the Yo-Yo Retrieve the lead-core shooting head drops to

the mud bottom. In some mountain lakes it would get tangled on a boulder or log strewn bottom.

The depth doesn't matter as long as a spot holds trout. Use the heavy lead-core line even in a few feet of water; the shooting line behind the lead core is always monofilament rather than floating running line. The leader varies from five to twelve feet, depending on the thickness of the weed beds—the heavier the weeds the longer the leader. The fly, a specially tied pattern with a foam underbody, such as a Floating Damsel, Floating Emergent Sparkle Pupa, or a Floating Marabou Single Egg, floats up over the weeds. With every strip of the retrieve the floating pattern dives and with every pause it bobs up, but the teasing action of the fly is only part of the Yo-Yo's effectiveness.

The other secret of the Yo-Yo is the lead-core line pulling through the weeds—not tearing them up but sending up puffs of mud and scaring out insects, crustaceans, leeches, and minnows. The heavy, lead-core shooting head creates a thirty-foot chum line as it slightly disturbs the bottom. This triggers feeding by the fish as the floating and diving fly swims right through them.

There are dozens of mountain lakes in my region with the right bottom characteristics for the Yo-Yo Retrieve. The specialized line and flies are worth carrying for rich waters because the technique often works on those dead fishing days when nothing else takes trout.

Leaders

My selection includes short leaders, three feet long tapering to 1X, for streamer fishing with sinking lines, and medium length leaders, seven to nine feet long tapering from 4X to 8X, for nymph fishing. I use the long leaders— up to eighteen feet long and carefully tapered for good turnover—for emerger and dry fly fishing.

My experiences on mountain lakes have made me very fussy about colored lines and long, hand-tied, perfectly tapered leaders for my surface fishing. There has been only one day when this "stealth" combination wasn't good enough. It was on Abicaulis Lake in the Clark Fork of the Columbia drainage:

Log entry: August 17th

Miracle of miracles—the wind is a curse on this little lake, not just blowing but always blowing hard, but today there was only a breeze. Over half of the lake was flat calm and trout were rising everywhere.

I paddled out in the kick boat and my passing didn't stop fish from feeding. Then I cast, the line settled on the water easily, and everything in a patch of ten square yards ran from the area. Not only did that circle in the lake go dead but it stayed dead. An hour later, with fish still dimpling everywhere else, nothing moved in that circle. I made two more casts, created two more empty zones, and started wishing for the return of the endless winds.

The only way I could take fish on a dry fly was by kicking over to the choppy water and casting back into the flat water. Even then the fly line had to land entirely in the chop; only the leader could touch the flat water without scattering these hypersensitive trout.

I used an eighteen-foot leader, which took some tinkering and tying to get it to turn over into the breeze that was blowing in my face. It had to be as long as possible to reach as far as possible into the flat water. Once the fly, a size-14 Shroud to match the *Callibaetis*, was into the middle of the feeding fish, it only took a few minutes to get a strike.

Chest Pack
* Predator Equipment Company

For hiking while fishing the chest pack works better with a backpack than a vest. Mine isn't overly stuffed, except with flies (which weigh next to nothing). Following are items you are likely to find in my chest pack:

- Binoculars (Orvis Image Stabilizer Binoculars)

- Fly Boxes (Sierra Pacific Bristle Tack Fly Boxes)
  Weight is always a consideration, and these are light.

- Fly Flotant (Loon Aquel or BT's Float-EZY)

- Gum Rubber Shock Material
  Dentists use this clear rubber material with braces. A 12-inch piece, tied with a double surgeon's knot between the butt section and the leader, cushions strikes and sudden lunges, preventing break-offs with fine tippets.

- Hook File
  This is for sharpening hooks, which should become a ritual before tying any fly onto the leader.

- Indicator Yarn
  This is for the Hang-and-Bob Technique. Black, which shows up in the silvery glare, and yellow are valuable colors on lakes.

- Leader Material (Maxima Chameleon from the butt section through 0X; and Umpqua for 1X through 8X)
  The properly tied dry-fly leader has a stiff butt, a fast-turning center, and a supple tippet. Even a nymph leader needs a supple tippet.

- Nippers

- Polaroid Sunglasses

- Split Shot

- Stomach Pump
  The name is misleading. The angler squeezes in a bit of water and sucks up the last few items a fish ate from his gullet. Properly used, the stomach pump goes nowhere near the stomach and doesn't injure a fish.

- Thermometer

What's missing? I leave out a lot of small accessories that are standard equipment in my regular fishing vest because every ounce counts; and a net is too bulky to carry into the high country.

MY FRIENDS would wake up screaming in the night at the thought of fishing a lake with only their river equipment. They are stillwater specialists, with rods, reels, lines, and leaders designed for the challenges posed by ponds and lakes. They also fish streams and rivers, but they use equipment designed to handle problems presented by running water.

Why don't stream specialists, who comprise the overwhelming majority of fly fishermen, have the same aversion to fishing a lake with only their river equipment? It doesn't seem to bother most of them. On any summer day on any popular Montana trout lake there are plenty of fly fishermen flailing away futilely with inappropriate gear. They catch little or nothing playing slog-and-flog.

The richer a lake, the more specialized you have to be to catch trout. Even on mountain waters, populated with supposedly unsophisticated wild fish, tactics developed specifically for stillwaters fool the most, the biggest, and the toughest residents. These specialized techniques require specialized equipment. Consistent success in lakes start with the proper tackle.

CHAPTER 9

July 19th — No-trail hikes; hitting the bonanza

PUTTING the backpack on, shifting it and getting the
weight settled, is a great moment. Feeling it is an affirma-
tion of strength, a simple statement of defiance against
aging. My body says, "I can carry this."

Putting the backpack on feels almost as good as slipping
it off. Real hikers never take the pack off during rest stops.
They sit propped against a rock or tree to relieve the weight.
The best moment for dropping it is at the end, after arriving
at the campsite. Just to release the bite of the straps on the
shoulders and the pull of the bag on the back brings a deli-
cious cessation of discomfort. It's euphoric.

There's one feeling I crave more than lifting a backpack on or sliding it off. It comes the moment I step off the trail, compass in hand, and head cross-country for a lake that has no path to it. The excitement is partly the adrenaline rush from the risk. The danger is real and the fear of falling and getting hurt or of straying and getting lost sits like a cold lump inside me. This feeling is a primitive, instinctive warning system in most humans, compelling us to weigh the risks.

Males tend to ignore it. My friend, Stan Bradshaw, calls this lack of caution "testosterone poisoning—a leading cause of death in young men." Of course, by my age I should be smarter, more cautious, but I just wonder why we should be more afraid of death when we have fewer years to lose. We are; and this explains why old men don't fight in wars. Males stop feeling bulletproof at around age thirty-five. I go to high-mountain lakes that don't have trails into them anyway. Hopefully the trip will be with a hiking buddy, because a companion is an element of safety, but at least half the time no one can go or no one wants to go, so I leave a schedule and a detailed map of my destination with a friend and walk in by myself.

LIGHTNING AND I had no bad history, not even a scare in spite of all the thunderstorms I had fished through in the fifties and sixties. I wouldn't avoid those black clouds. I'd rush out and start casting just as the wind began kicking the water into a chop, the rain began landing in fat drops, and the bolts began thumping on the hill tops around me. The fishing was always incredible.

In the early seventies my fishing partner, Stan Bradshaw, had the good sense to avoid all lightning. As a boy he'd had a bolt hit the path just ahead of him, catching him in the blue flash and knocking him on his rear. On our fishing trips he got nervous anytime the air became charged—and his fear was contagious. He'd say it was respect, not fear, but I know when I'm scared and being around him and lightning made me a quivering marshmallow.

My own close encounters with lightning began on a trip in the Flathead area. On a cross-country trek I reached a ridgeline, a bare jumble of rock at least a half mile long, late in the afternoon. The predictable mountain wind that sweeps from the valley to the mountain top and creates thunderstorms, was already flowing up the slope. The breezes almost crackled with static.

I didn't want to wait in the safe area within the trees until the storm was over. I started scrambling over and around the boulders, calling my two dogs, Chester and Zeb, to keep them close. When I was a hundred yards into the ridgeline the storm broke. It was my first storm right up on the mountain top. No lightning storm in the valley could ever match the ferocity of this one. The wind kicked and the rain fell, but as bad as both of these were, they were hardly noticeable at that moment. The lightning strikes hit so fast all around us that it was impossible to hear the individual thunderclap that I associate with a strike. The ozone was so thick, so gagging, that it was difficult to breathe. I dove for a spot against a car-sized boulder, pulling a tarpaulin over me and calling in the dogs.

Zeb, my fearless Rottweiler, barked at each strike and then, turning left and right, barked at the echoes of thunder. Chester, more afraid of loud noises, lay flat and shook, but when I held him and talked softly into his ear he stopped quivering, just staring into my face, his faith firm in my ability to quench lightning. The three of us huddled under the tarp, pummeled by the wind and rain and noise; and there was a picture in my head of the fried mess we would make if we got blasted by one of the bolts.

The human mind gets used to anything, even the numbing fear that forced me to my knees and left me clinging to that boulder with my dogs. After a half hour of crouching on that mountain ridge, flinching from more lightning flashes than I'd see in a year in the valley, I started to think about running for the forest on the far side. It was time for me to pee, if nothing else, so I stood up in the rain—there's something empowering about pissing on a mountain alive with electricity and surviving. With my dogs, I climbed through and over the boulder field as fast as possible to the safety of the trees.

I kept moving, ignoring the soaking rain, because I wanted to find this hidden, no-trail lake before dark. A mile across country took an hour, instead of the usual twenty minutes or so it takes on a trail. There were long stops to check the compass, read the topo map, and pick out another landmark ahead. I didn't stop pushing hard until I topped a crest and saw the glint of water from the Fire Lakes.

IN MONTANA there is an abundance of trout waters, but these days they are all getting more anglers. At times I enjoy the conviviality of the crowds on the Bighorn, the Madison, or the Missouri, but more often I want some solitude. So I go to valley lakes when the rivers get busy, to high-mountain lakes when the valley lakes get busy, and to no-trail lakes when the more accessible mountain lakes get busy.

The most accessible high-mountain trout waters are popular in the middle of the summer. Good fishing lakes within ten miles of the trailhead usually get a dozen or more hikers on a weekend; and on any lake, no matter how distant, there are almost always private parties with their horses and sometimes commercial horse outfitters with up to twenty fishermen.

The only way to be alone is by going across rough, trailess terrain. The distance and the fear of getting lost stops normal hikers. The trailess ground stops packers, all except goat packers. And for me, if the reason for going to a lake is solitude, why bring a fishing partner? If I need to be alone for a few days, it's worth the risk of going with just my dogs.

I can name my favorite no-trail lakes with no fear of attracting a crowd. I can scream the glories of my perfect waters in western Montana—George Lake, in the South Fork of the Flathead drainage, with an incredibly steep, two-mile, no-trail climb up and over a mountain, for lonely westslope cutthroats; Wee Lake, in the Kootenai drainage, only a mile bushwhack but easy to miss because it's so small, for 16- to 22-inch trout; or Ducharme Lake, in the Swan River drainage, so remote it's not even named on the maps, for its abundant 18-inch cutthroats. Sometimes it feels like these lakes were put there just for me; and sometimes the simplest way to find great fishing is to outwork everyone else.

I picked my way down the last half mile of hill to the three Fire Lakes, knowing that the fishing might not match the rumors of big brookies, but not really caring at the moment. When my tent was set up on the middle lake, and a fire was popping in the dusk, it was time to stare out at the water and count rises. In the last moments of twilight, when the rain stopped, the lake surface was broken by rolling fish.

Early the next morning, even before stringing my rod, I walked around the lake and looked into the water trying to spot fish. The bigger brookies were easy to see—they always are the easiest trout to spot because they're dark and the white edges of their fins flash clearly.

They weren't easy to catch. The fish didn't like movement, flushing even before the line hit the water. I had to build a longer leader, stretching it out to sixteen feet, to get a fly in front of them. But they didn't fuss over pattern, rising freely to an assortment of dry flies and taking any wet fly or nymph. They were unsophisticated, not because they were brookies, but because they were true wilderness trout, most probably seeing a fake insect for the first time.

At first my goal was to catch fish, but after landing a number of them from 11 to 16 inches long, my search for larger fish began in earnest. I climbed high on a rock, watching for the biggest swirls, and when a nice brookie rose, I cast quickly to the area.

My toughest cast was to a cruiser coming along the shoreline, appearing suddenly right below me. I parachuted line above me and let it collapse in a pile on the water. The dry fly fluttered down perfectly, away from the heap of line. The trout, the biggest fish of the morning, easily 18 inches, sucked in the imitation. I didn't wait for him to close his mouth or turn down, lifting straight up on the strike and pulling the hook away without nicking so much as a lip.

For a moment, just a moment, sitting there laughing at the dumbest of moves, I wished I had a friend along to share the giggle with.

IT FELT GOOD being alone on the Fire Lakes, with no trash or old fire rings to remind me of people. Because I was alone, I slept when I wanted, ate when I wanted, and fished when I wanted. Over the three days I caught seventy or eighty brook trout, a few topping 16 inches, but most of my time was spent finding spring holes, noting concentrations of fish, sampling bottom fauna, examining the stomach contents of my few breakfast trout, and sketching crude maps of the three lakes.

On the fourth day I woke up early, packed quickly, and hiked hard to the exposed ridgeline, getting there long before the afternoon thunderheads started vibrating. I looked at the blue sky and saw nothing but a few wispy, white clouds. I still crossed that rock field in a mad scramble.

I called Bernie Samuelson, who was holding my destination map and waiting for me to check in, as soon as I got home. "Those lakes were beautiful, Bernie."

"How was the fishing?"

"A bonanza. I found the bonanza of big brook trout."

He wailed, as only he could, in anguish, and said, "I wish I could have been there."

"I almost died up there, Bernie. I was on a ridge in the craziest lightning storm you've ever seen."

"I wish I could have been there," he said again, and he meant it.

I sent some friends into the Fire Lakes. They refused to leave the creek bottom at the high meadow and strike out up hill through the tangle of downed trees, like they were supposed to, and they never found the ridgeline, the halfway marker on the trip into these waters. After three days of wandering the jumble of valleys in this wild section of the Flathead River drainage, they gave up the hunt and came out wet, cold, and beaten. They promised that they'd never try again.

CHAPTER 10

The Magic Winds of Summer

THIS SUMMER there are ants in my kitchen. They crawl up the pipes under the sink and start across the linoleum. When my Rottweiler puppy sees them he pounces and licks them up. No one is in any rush to get rid of the ants. At the moment they're saving me money on dog food and the kitchen floor is getting cleaned.

You combine ants and anabatic winds and you have the summer secret to mountain lakes.

DURING THE SUMMER terrestrial insects are important on most kinds of waters. But on high-mountain lakes they

are more than important—without them there might not
even be fishable populations of trout in these harsh habitats. In virtually every food study terrestrials make up 80
percent or more of the summer diet of trout and grayling in
alpine environments.

The numbers are so skewed towards terrestrials that it
seems like the science must be flawed. All the other food
sources in high lakes become an afterthought in the daily
feeding routine. This would be impossible if terrestrials
were just random—impossible if ants, beetles, leafhoppers,
and grasshoppers simply blunder in along the shore or get
blown in by stray gusts of wind moving through the grass or
trees. Terrestrials couldn't constitute 80 percent of the summer diet without a predictable and dependable delivery system unique to mountain terrain.

John Breitenger, a pilot, described a flight in the mountains in his private plane, "We were going from Livingston
to Fort Smith, staying at 13,000 feet, well above the peaks,
and we'd pass through columns of bugs and the windshield
would get splattered so badly, so gooed up, that we'd have
to scrub it clean every time we landed."

Those insects aren't carried up thousands of feet by stray
gusts—they are lifted with the incredible force of anabatic
winds that rush up the mountain slopes like the air up a
chimney. On days with weak winds, lighter insects—ants
and leafhoppers—are swept upwards; on days with strong
winds, beetles and even grasshoppers also are carried aloft.

One of the secrets of mountain lakes is that the vertical
winds, not horizontal ones, deposit most of the food on the
water. The other secret is that the trout in these lakes, given
a choice, prefer to feed on the surface.

IT ISN'T SURPRISING that trout in a high-mountain lake
cruise and search for food items on the top. Most of these

waters are pretty infertile. The primary production of single-celled organisms is low; rooted plants are often entirely absent. Two-winged flies, mainly Diptera midges, are the most abundant aquatic insect, but larger aquatic forms can be scarce. There are no major hatches of mayflies, caddisflies, or damselflies on many of these waters. Terrestrials falling onto the surface are a precious gift for high-mountain trout.

But the preference for top feeding isn't just a habit of trout on infertile lakes. There are numerous scientific studies that show a real prejudice *against* subsurface browsing even in rich lakes. These same studies suggest that fish are sitting on the bottom just waiting for something to pop up to or drop onto the top. Combine terrestrial insects and emergent or adult forms of aquatic insects and the amount of food taken at the surface climbs to over 90 percent in some months.

This is the implication of a report by J. N. Ball about Llyn Tegid, a three-square mile lake in Wales that certainly fits into the "rich valley water" category. In his paper, "On the Food of the Brown Trout of Llyn Tegid," the author broke his research on the feeding habits of brown trout into two periods:

OCTOBER THROUGH APRIL
trout fed mainly on bottom-living organisms

MAY THROUGH SEPTEMBER
trout fed mainly at the surface

May = 88% surface food

June = 78% surface food

July = 59% surface food

August = 59% surface food

September = 95% surface food

According to J. N. Ball's samplings, during the summer months when top and bottom food were equally available, the trout strongly preferred to feed on items either in or on the surface film. The fish focused on the rich fare of fresh-water shrimp and insect larvae and nymphs in the bottom weeds only during the cold-weather months when they had no choice.

The reason is vulnerability—always a more important determinant of feeding than relative abundance. So what if the weeds and bottom gravel are crammed with crayfish, scuds, aquatic worms, leeches, and insect larvae and nymphs? Those organisms are relatively safe in their natural sanctuaries from fish. Any food item perched in or on the surface film, outlined against the sky, is totally exposed. And with terrestrials there's no chance the insect is going to fly away.

THERE ARE FOUR primary delivery systems for moving terrestrials from the land to the water. One is barely significant, another is sporadic, a surprising one is constant, and the most important is a mystery.

The runoff from a rainstorm is barely significant as a method of transport. The water washes over the land, especially during a cloudburst, gathers in rivulets, and runs into the lake. These trickles carry a load of drowned organisms, spiders and worms as well as all kinds of insects. There always seem to be bees—both real ones and the two-winged flies that are disguised in the same color scheme—and there are plenty of ants and beetles in the mix. During a heavy storm, the outlets of temporary rivulets and swollen tributaries attract trout, which feed along the edge of the mud line. This runoff is too random to provide a large percentage of all the terrestrials that end up in a lake, but it can be important during a storm.

The sporadic transport system is horizontal wind, those gusts waving the treetops. The stronger the breeze the more likely it is to push insects over the lake and scatter them on the surface. A prime place to fish is from the lee shore, where there's a band of calm water. The best place to cast a fly is right where the ripple line starts on the lake. These regular winds put enough insects on the water to be a significant part of terrestrial dispersal, but they're not as important as you might think. They're not the primary source of blow-ins.

Even what I call the "blunder effect" contributes more food to a lake than regular winds. During summer months flying terrestrials blunder onto the water constantly, day and night, for no apparent reason. This is simply accidental drowning, with no outside agent, such as wind, to explain it. It actually happens more when there is no wind because insects fly more in calm conditions. To test this phenomenon put a pan of water out for twenty-four hours. At the end of the time there'll be flies, bees, moths, and other flying insects drowned in the pan. The surface area of the pan is minuscule compared to the surface area of a lake; and in our screen samplings on mountain waters, flying terrestrials of all kinds, in some suicidal drive, kept touching down on and getting mired in the surface.

The first three methods by which terrestrials land on a lake still account for less than 50 percent of the total. All three don't equal the impact of anabatic winds on terrestrial insects. The chimney effect sucks air up thousands of feet. This phenomenon deposits so many organisms on the water, predictably and dependably, that fisheries biologists even have a name for the victims—upslope blow-ins. And any fly fisherman who understands this process can take advantage of the feeding activity it triggers in fish.

THE STORM never broke that afternoon, but it seemed so imminent that I sat there with my raincoat on for two hours. A stranger hiking the trail around Pear Lake stopped next to me and looked out at the water at the man bobbing up and down on the chop. "Who's he?"

"Bernie Samuelson."

For a long time he just watched my buddy out on the lake in the kick boat and he didn't say anything. Finally he asked, "Isn't he the guy with the goat?"

"They say the goat's the smart one."

"That's what I heard," he said, and headed up the path.

The first day was a failure. It was overcast and chilly even for early July; and nothing happened. During his shift on the water, sitting in one kick boat and watching two others lashed together and covered with a white sheet, Bernie periodically called to me, "Bugs. Bugs. I want bugs."

We had the equipment to test for anabatic winds— white linen and kick boats and collection vials. What we lacked was a meteorologist. It would have been nice if either one of us had even a basic understanding of wind dynamics. We didn't—we were going on faith that vertical air movement and insect deposition were real.

After seven hours watching a sheet stay clean enough to serve dinner on, our faith was badly shaken. No bugs fell and we didn't know why. There were no insect blow-ins of any kind. The few rainbow trout that were rising in the bay were splashing for adult egg-laying midges. None of the fish caught and kept for a camp supper had any terrestrials in the upper half of the gut.

The next day was clear. It started cold, with a skim of frost on our tent, but it quickly warmed up. By the afternoon it was hot for the mountains, with an air temperature of 74 degrees Fahrenheit. At exactly 3:07 p.m. Bernie, again watching the white sheet, started whooping. Insects were falling on the linen and on the water.

Dimples like raindrops pocked the lake, but it was sunny and there was no rain. Soon trout were sipping and cruising in zigzag fashion, hunting for fallen insects. They continued to feed steadily on terrestrials for nearly three hours, until early evening, when they switched to a hatch of cinnamon caddisflies.

At the end of the day Bernie tallied what he had collected from the white sheet: nineteen insects total in three hours (thirteen wingless ants, one beetle, one leafhopper, and, in Bernie's words, four "strange six-legged creatures").

Why had the insects fallen the second day and not the first? Why did it happen in the afternoon and not in the morning? A little of that meteorological knowledge about winds would have saved us hours of futile observation. There are times when anabatic winds aren't going to happen in these mountains—they're very predictable.

I spent my first day out of the mountains at the University of Montana library with those meteorology books.

IT'S WRONG TO THINK of anabatic winds as shooting straight up into the atmosphere. They don't—they're "up-slope" winds. They happen in the mountains. The air follows the contour of the land, hugging the slope and sweeping up insects from rocks, grasses, and trees.

Air temperature variations cause wind. When the air is the same temperature over a wide area there isn't much movement. On a normal day winds are weakest in the morning and strongest in the afternoon. Anabatic winds happen on warm, sunny days in the afternoon.

The terrain has to be right for anabatic winds, but any time a lake is closely surrounded by mountains the terrain is perfect. The upslope effect occurs when the high ridges receive the morning sun. The tops of the mountains heat up, while the valley floor is still shaded. On a normal day the temperature difference increases until early afternoon. Then the cool air of the valley is sucked up to the mountain ridges as layers mix and equalize. The greater the temperature disparity between mountain top and valley bottom the stronger the wind.

In September we went back to Pear Lake, nearly 8,500 feet up in the Crazies, and repeated the early season experiment. After a below freezing morning the day turned warm. By two o'clock, when we launched and anchored the kick boats, the winds were already pulsing upwards through the treetops. The bugs started dropping at 3:14 p.m., a much heavier fall than in July. In three hours fifty-five creatures landed on the linen—eighteen ants, four grasshoppers, twelve beetles, seven leafhoppers, ten "strange six-legged creatures", and four non-insects. Fish fed heavily on the surface.

Ants are one of the organisms that seem to lift easiest in the winds. On a day with mild upslope breezes they're often the overwhelming insect on the lake. Sometimes spiders, not an insect but always present in the high country, make up a major percentage of the blow-ins. Occasionally the winds hit a concentration of a single kind of insect, an odd-ball type that isn't around other times, and anything from lacewings to butterflies can be important. The organisms fall vertically, like rain from the sky. The source of the blow-ins can be a thousand or more feet below the ridges. Frequently the organisms come from even lower valleys, or from the base of the mountain range. They fall because of uneven mixing in the atmosphere. In the swirling air currents, with some gusts reversing into downslope winds, any wingless or weak-flying insects are at the mercy of thermal variations. A lake is a heat sink, much cooler than the surrounding land by late afternoon on a sunny summer day. This explains why so many creatures drop onto the water.

There is an opposite to upslope winds. From late afternoon into night the valley loses sunlight to shadows. It cools faster than the ridges. The air flow reverses—strong downslope winds follow the contours of the mountains. These winds also knock weak-flying insects, such as winged ants and termites, onto the water. The falls of migrating insects onto lakes and even big rivers aren't pure chance either.

WITH TERRESTRIAL INSECTS dropping from the sky dependably and predictably on warm afternoons, high-mountain lakes suddenly start to look like dry fly paradise. The mystery is that fly fishermen don't perceive the high lakes this way. Anglers bring boxes of streamers, wet flies, nymphs, and woolly buggers to the mountains. Friends who hike with me seem surprised that my selection is mostly emergers and dry flies. My assortment of patterns—eleven dry flies, three emergers, seven nymphs, two wet flies, two streamers, and one egg fly—reflects the foraging habits of high-country trout.

Wild fish in hard-to-reach waters can get finicky when there's a hatch of aquatic insects busting out all over. They'll key on midges, mayflies, caddisflies, or damselflies; and my boxes contain matches for all stages of these insects. They'll focus strictly on flying ants and flying termites when the migration flights dump large numbers of these insects. But the same trout feed unselectively on the terrestrials that fall with the upslope winds on the water. The fish cruise, taking an ant here and a beetle there, accepting whatever is next on the path. They get used to seeing a variety of sizes, shapes, and colors in the hodge-podge of insects that end up mired and helpless on the surface.

In our six experiments counting upslope blow-ins, ants were the predominant organism every time; and beetles were the second most abundant insect every time. Either an ant or a beetle imitation works consistently on fish sipping terrestrials. My favorite patterns are two ants, a size-16 Red Foam Ant and a size-8 Black Flying Foam Ant, a size-14 Green Foam Beetle, or, for those days when spiders are abundant in the collections, a size-14 Brown Foam Spider. As a "shock" attractor/imitation, for making large trout rush up from the depths to smack something, there's always a size-12 Deer Hair Hornet in my box.

What's happened to me since discovering these anabatic winds on my high lakes? The work taught me to look for the upslope blow-ins on warm afternoons. The experiments taught me that insects fall erratically on a lake, sometimes over one area and not another, and that at the first sign of active feeding by the fish it's important to paddle madly to get to the spot. The knowledge gave me the faith to fish a dry fly in choppy water when it's impossible to see rising trout.

These anabatic winds have made me a lazier fisherman. If trout are not rising, I'll sit and wait for the afternoon breezes. I know where the fish rest when they're not actually feeding—most of them hold at the drop-off just beyond the shallows. But I'll sit on the shore, my kick boat inflated and my rod strung up, just listening for the soft hissing of the upslope winds curling through the trees.

CHAPTER 11

*August 4th — The World's Smartest Fishing
Dog (#2); the Slough Pig and a monster brown*

AT SOME POINT it's going to sound like I am picking
on Labrador retrievers, but I am not. They are great dogs.
Chester is just one of those one-in-a-million "Einstein"
freaks that breaks norms. He understands the nature of
competition, and although he would never view himself as
the underdog in retrieving, everyone else does. The Major
got some perverted pleasure out of having Chester outper-
form champion Labradors. And so do I.

Strangely enough, Chester (a German shepherd/mutt
cross) didn't have the strong instinct to retrieve. He had to

be taught how to do it. A friend, Kenny Pope, was at my house with his two black Labradors. I'd throw a stick and the Labs would run out to get it. Chester just sat there.

"Chester, you can do this," I said.

I threw the stick again. Chester didn't move, but when the black Labs came running back and dropped the stick, he picked it up, ran out, and dropped it for them. One of the Labradors beat the other to the stick and retrieved it. Chester trotted back and gave me a look that said, "How long are we going to keep playing silly games with these dogs?"

The two black Labs stood there panting, their look saying, "Come on, Chester. Huh, Chester? Drop it again, Chester. Huh, Chester?"

The Major was more than just intrigued by Chester's retrieving skills. He liked him in a way he didn't like most dogs because my dog never fawned for affection. He was friendly enough, but Chester looked everyone, including the Major at his gruffest, in the eyes as if the person was at least an equal.

The Major began inviting me in for coffee before I'd go fishing. He would harangue more than talk. Like many people who've lived on government money all their lives he was a firm believer in conservative principles, and since it was his pond out back and I'm a firm believer in little except fishing, I'd sit and listen.

One day the Major brought Chester into the kitchen with us. The Major's daughter came in with coffee and saw my mongrel lying on the floor near her father's chair. She glared at me, not realizing who had done the inviting, and said, "We don't allow dogs in the house."

The Major said, "That's Chester, and he's not just any dog, Cillia. He's my guest and you should apologize to him," and Chester looked at her, ignoring the dog biscuit the Major was trying to slip him, until she did say she was sorry.

The Major has all sorts of friends from the big retrieving trials. These people have winning Labrador retrievers with long names and lengthy lineages. We all go out to the pond and the Major points out a little quirk about Labs, "Lucky this is a short pond. If that dog had to swim any farther, we'd be here after dark."

Labradors are slow, on land and in water. They move like overloaded tugboats when they swim. Chester is fast, sixty pounds of flash. He's only a step or two slower than a greyhound on land. In the water his front paws, his back paws, and even his swishing tail all pound furiously to drive him forward.

After the "speed test," with Chester easily winning any race, these people with the Labradors always insist on throwing out more than one retrieving dummy. They're so predictable. They toss a couple of dummies and the Labrador gets one and then the other. The dog sits there panting and the owner stands there grinning. As if this is the height of canine glory. Dog and owner—at that moment I'm not sure which one is modeling for a statue of the Village Idiot.

Then the Major sets Chester and throws five or six dummies—in the cattail swamp, over islands, out in the open water. Chester watches him toss, and then one by one with no direction signals he goes and gets them. And he's fast.

The Major's favorite trick is the "beaver stick." We collect and save peeled, water-logged, beaver-chopped sticks. The Major throws one for a Labrador and the dog swims out and can't find it and the owner whines, "That's not fair. It sank."

The peeled stick is sort of "neutral density." It doesn't sink all the way, suspending in three to five feet of water, and it's white. Chester swims to the area, dives and disappears, and comes up with the stick.

"Damn," the Labrador owner says, more like a compliment than a curse, as Chester swims in.

"Yes, sir," the Major says, "that's my buddy, the World's Smartest Dog."

CHESTER SPOTS FISH, not just white, beaver-peeled sticks. He knows enough to run up a hill, or stand up on a boat seat, to took down into the water. He has seen every big fish my friends and I have stalked on the different ponds in my valley. He just stares where I stare.

July 3 — 14-pound 2-ounce brown trout (my largest to date) from the Hog Hole at the Settling Ponds; three other browns over 5 pounds.

July 12 — An 8-pound brown on a Rollover Scud (first fish on this new fly) from Jones Pond.

July 23 — For some reason the browns were cruising among the sunken iron scrap of the old mining machinery at the Gold Creek Dredge Ponds. For three hours I landed every fish under 18 inches and lost every one over 18 inches. Finally, one of the real big ones, after sucking in a sinking Twist Nymph, ran for open water instead diving for the metal tangle and I caught him, a 4-pound 7-ounce brown.

August 22 — I was with Robert Ince, from England, on the Hog Hole; he caught two browns over 5 pounds and seven rainbows over 3 pounds. My biggest brown was 7 pounds plus and there was a cutthroat of 3 pounds, a rarity in the Settling Ponds.

September 14 — I was fishing on the Job Corps ponds, the first one in the string of four dug-out holes.

What happened? These ponds are only three years old; they weren't stocked until last year and there aren't supposed to be any big fish in them yet. A brown trout must have washed in with high water from one of the feeder streams and grew fast on a diet of hatchery rainbows. He took a size-14 Clear Wing Gray Spinner, a match for the *Callibaetis* the smaller fish were sipping, and in the weighnet he scaled 6 pounds 15 ounces.

September 18 — I caught my second largest trout ever, an 11-pound fish. It was in the Hog Hole, right in the ditch in front of the outflow pipe, exactly where the 14-pound brown was earlier.

The problem with every pond in the Deer Lodge valley is that the biggest fish are brown trout. There are differences between the browns and the rainbows, cutthroats, and brookies in these waters. The differences are critical ones for an angler trying to spot brown trout. The browns cruise and feed on the same food as other trout, and they'll take the same flies presented in the same ways in stillwaters, but brown trout have three quirks:

1) They often cruise deeper than rainbows during the day, and are harder to spot;
2) They cruise and feed in shallow areas near dark and into the night, long after rainbows have settled down for the evening;
3) They spook more easily than rainbows, especially if they're in those shallow areas.

One of my regular partners for the valley stillwaters, Joel Hart, and I developed one solution for the problem of deep-cruising fish. We chipped in together and bought an old aluminum john boat. Then we welded an 8-foot stepladder to the boat's floor.

That stepladder is our observation deck. One of us stands near the top rung and searches for trout while the other rows slowly across the pond or lake. When the spotter sees a fish, the man on the oars picks up the fly rod and casts where he is told to cast.

Pity the fisherman who misses a cruiser. Joel screams, "I said twenty-five feet at four o'clock. Four o'clock. Not one-thirty, you moron."

"My watch is slow."

He moans and hits his head against the ladder, "I'm getting me a new partner."

Those deep-cruising fish can be chumps. No angler at water level can ever see them. The trout feel safe in eight to twelve feet of water. Food is not quite as plentiful among the patchy weeds of the deeper areas in our local ponds, and the browns actually seem less selective than the rainbows.

The virtue of this method is obvious: no blind flogging. Once we see a fish and observe his path, the path he will follow time after time, we usually hook him. Our best catches occur during the middle of the day under bright sun with flat, calm water—not what most fly fishermen would call the magic hours. The downside is that our boat, dubbed the "Slough Pig," is not the most seaworthy of crafts.

I recorded one of our adventures in my August 4 log entry:

> The Major is so fond of Chester that not only can I come out anytime, but I can bring along any fishing buddy. This has made me a lot more popular in my hometown. I'm thinking of running for political office.
>
> Joel and I launched the "Slough Pig" and we started circling the pond looking for cruisers. There are only browns here, and to my knowledge it hasn't been stocked in fifteen years, enough fish spawning successfully in a

spring feeder to replenish the water. The pond was not crystal clear, the growth of weed and algae making a few sections impossible for spotting, but at the far end against the one steep bank we saw shapes crossing the light sand bottom.

The Major came down and sat on his bench. He called for Chester and threw sticks out on the pond, but as much as Chester loves to fetch, he loves to fish more and he ignored the fuss. He perched up on the front of the boat and stared down into the water as hard as Joel stared down from his position on the ladder. Whether or not he could see the trout I don't know, but when Joel began huffing, choking, and hyperventilating, before finally blurting something about a whale, Chester leaned out to see better. I stood up to see better and spotted the big brown feeding about twenty-five feet out to my left (he was bigger than the seven trout that we'd already caught that morning, bigger than the fourteen-pounder I'd caught on the Settling Ponds, and even bigger than the brown that had followed my streamer all the way to the boat in New Zealand, a fish that had the guide hoarsely whispering a weight in kilos that translated to more than sixteen pounds).

I made a cast so perfect that not even Joel could yell about it. The fly landed far enough ahead of the trout to sink just in front of the big boy's face. I gave the Bristle Leech a small twitch and the fish started accelerating. Watching him come like that, I just naturally went into that hunched up, forward lean as I got ready to set the hook. Chester also leaned out a little further, and up there on the ladder, screaming Joel leaned way out, and I'm not sure if I first heard or felt the cold wash on my feet, but I looked down at water coming in over the side of the tilted boat.

Chester jumped clear, but I ignored him. Joel held on as the boat floundered, ready to go down with the ship, but I ignored him. I've never been so steady in a crisis; my heart colder than a politician's—and I just kept waiting for that trout to reach and suck in the fly. I was falling, pitching headlong, when he took the Bristle Leech, but I kept my focus. I tried with every muscle to set the hook, twisting in the air to push the rod back. There was no force to the set, and I knew it, stripping in line and yanking repeatedly even when I was in the water, hoping he still had the hook in his mouth.

Chester abandoned us, swimming up on the shore and running over to the Major. We grabbed the sides of the Slough Pig, now turned over, with the ladder pointing straight down, and tried to kick with it over to the shallows, but it sank completely. Joel snatched the rope before it sank and swam with it to shore.

The Major was laughing so hard he was down on the bench, rocking in a fetal position, and all he could say as we sloshed up was, "You boys are worth the price of admission." But we didn't care about the Major; and for the moment we didn't care about the boat or the tackle on the pond bottom. All we could talk about was the size of that brown trout.

"The Three Stooges go fishing," the Major added, and only Chester had enough pride to look insulted. Joel and I just shrugged.

In all our years of fish-spotting in ponds and lakes, we've never failed to catch a particular trout once we knew about him. The story about going out day after day to the same spot to fool a huge trout in a stream or river is a fly fishing truism—it's possible and with enough persistence it's almost inevitable if that trout doesn't migrate or die. The same obsession with one fish is just as possible in a pond or lake. Maybe success is even more inevitable because a trout in stillwater will never move far from his home area. A trout in a pond or lake is a creature of habit, and the food-rich environment of the limestone ponds in our valley makes any fish stay-at-home lazy.

CHAPTER 12

Summer Strategies

DURING SPRING and fall even heavy hatches of midges—the first and last insects to emerge each season—don't guarantee rising trout. It's not just water temperature, but the direction the water temperature is moving, that seems to determine the activity level of fish. After a few warm days trout feed freely. After a few nasty days, even if they have been gorging on midge pupae and adults before the cold snap, the same fish might ignore insects on top. The dropping water temperatures drive trout into deeper water.

A particularly discouraging incident of "cold-weather lockjaw" happened on lower Dolus Lake in June (which is still springtime in the Rockies). The lake was fishing well according to reports, but three days of rain and three nights of sub-freezing temperatures cooled the water considerably. By the time John Heller and I hiked up there the surface fishing was all over. This wasn't for lack of insects—a size-16, olive-bodied midge was popping out all over the shallows. Nothing but small fish rose to the big midges. It was strange to see so much food riding the surface with nothing really happening. John had to tie on a beadhead nymph and use an ultraslow retrieve to catch a decent-sized trout.

But this is in the spring. When summer begins stringing out warm, dry days, the surface fishing becomes much more consistent. Short-term temperature drops don't bother the trout. Dry flies and emergers work when they're supposed to work—and the most dependable situations are when insects are on the water.

IN THE SUMMER on mountain lakes the search for fish feeding on the surface begins right at the edge. An angler who rushes up to the water probably won't see trout streaking for the depths. If he does, he might wonder what those fish were doing within a few feet of the shore. The trout weren't cruising, not in the normal swim-and-hunt fashion, and they probably weren't feeding on nymphs.

Dry-fly fishing on lakes starts at the compression zone next to the bank. Waves, especially with a wind driving the water, hit the land and wash back out, a miniature version of ocean breakers pounding a beach. The next wave and the splash of the last wave kicking out collide, catching and compressing all the flotsam, everything from pine needles to drowned insects. A scum line forms along the bank, the distance out depending on wind strength.

Andy Stahl plays an old dry-fly game with me. We take turns dapping, and with our 12-foot rods the method is as deadly on lakes as it is on streams. We use bushes, tree trunks, and boulders for cover and slowly scan the water. If we find no fish in an area, we quickly move to a different hiding place. Once we find a trout, one of us touches a dry fly on the water. We let the pattern hang straight down from the rod tip, putting a split shot on the leader a few feet above the fly on a windy day.

Last summer Andy dressed in drab clothes, taking off every shiny geegaw, such as his wedding ring, watch, and wire-rimmed glasses. He put paste wax on the shaft and guides to dull the shine of his fly rod. He crept with soft steps in a crouch along the shore. His success rate was impressive.

The best time for dapping seems to be on summer mornings, while the chill is still in the air and before any hatches really start to appear. The trout nose the scum-line debris, looking for the drowned remnants of the previous night's insect activity. They can become so fussy about the fly, especially when there are so many drowned, egg-laying microcaddis littering the water, that size becomes a selective feature. Generally, however, a small Foam Beetle is a good, all-around choice, being bright enough, with its wide wing of translucent packing foam, to stand out among the flotsam and pull fish to it.

MY SUMMER STRATEGIES on mountain lakes focus on surface techniques with dry flies or emergers. The early morning means stalking the bank. At midmorning, and then again in the early afternoon, there are often midge, damselfly, and mayfly hatches. The late afternoon winds, sweeping up the slopes on warm days, drop the daily bonanza of terrestrial insects. Evening is emergence and egg-laying time again, with caddisflies often the most important insects on the surface.

During the summer, if there's a time when surface flies won't work on mountain lakes, it's often at midday. With flat water, under a bright sky, the fish either stay deep or hide under cover. Trout don't have to drop down very far to be safe from diving birds. They usually hang on the sharp drop-off beyond the littoral shelf. The Multiple-Roll technique with a leech imitation can bring these fish to the surface.

Any downed timber in a bay or along the shore hides non-feeding trout. You can spot them among the shadows. The trick is to drop a nymph accurately in a hole and let the fly sink to the bottom. There usually isn't space for a long retrieve, and often a retrieve isn't necessary. A fly sitting on the mud apparently has its own appeal, and a trout, if it sees the fly settle, will often come over and suck an inert nymph off the bottom. If the "sit-and-wait" routine doesn't work, the slightest pull, not enough to even lift the fly but just enough to stir silt, will usually make a fish rush to the fly.

It is odd how my friends specialize. Bernie Samuelson hits lakes at ice-out. Joel Hart works at spotting fish. Ken Mira fishes nymphs deep with sinking lines. Ron Ruddig spaces as many as four flies on a leader, the bottom one as deep as twelve feet, for the Hang-and-Bob technique. My favorite fishing on mountain lakes happens during the hatches.

Midges

Taff Price, in the English work, *Tying and Fishing the Nymph*, points out a situation when even burrowing midge larvae are available to trout. "On lakes and reservoirs, after a period of windy weather, the mud of the shoreline is often churned up by the action of wind and wave, and creatures such as chironomids, that live in the mud are washed out of their chambers and hiding-holes. Trout often patrol these muddy margins in search of such 'wash-out' food."

The pupal and adult stages of the midge aren't as dominant during the summer as during early spring and late fall, but these insects are multibrooded, getting off more than one hatch a year, and the fly fishermen might find trout sipping emerging pupae or egg-laying adults anytime. Around dawn midges are most likely to be the only hatching insect.

The Halo Midge Emerger sits half in and half out of the surface film, but the exposed portion, with white foam pods and an orange spike, makes this pattern as easy to see as any dry fly. Even a small imitation stands out thirty feet away. It's usually better to fish two or even three of these flies at a time when trout are selectively locked onto the hatching insect. This multiple-fly approach is driven by the sheer numbers of naturals.

When adults are mixed on the surface with the pupae, a combination of an Improved Buzz Ball and a Halo Midge Emerger is more effective than a two-fly rig of either pattern. The Improved Buzz Ball, imitating a compact mass of mating insects during a swarm, draws the occasional smashing strike, but like any strong attractor it brings in curious trout for a look. Those same trout, after snubbing the attractor, typically sip any subtle imitation, such as the Halo Midge Emerger, that's in the vicinity.

Damsels

Gary Borger, in *Presentation*, compares the stillwater insect community with the running water insect community. "In lakes, damsels and dragons fill the ecological niche of the stonefly. Interestingly, the damsels and dragons share many characteristics with certain stoneflies. The damsels and dragons are big insects, they're fierce predators, they hatch on shore, and they stimulate the biggest fish to feed actively."

At times, even when water and weather seem perfect, trout refuse to rise for a very good reason—something more important is happening below the surface. Damselflies swim into the shallows during morning hours to emerge on reeds and sticks instead of popping up to the top of a lake. On a rich lake, with an abundance of aquatic weeds and a heavy population of damsels, trout concentrate on the migrating nymphs during a hatch, and nothing will bring those fish to the surface to feed. Species of the major dam-selfly genera, *Enallagma* and *Ischnura*, start emerging roughly a week after their main food source, mosquitoes, become a problem for anglers.

The best retrieve for mimicking damsel nymphs is three steady pulls on the line, done so smoothly that the imita-tion never stops swimming, and then a short pause. After each pause shake the fly line back out of the rod guides in a retro-strip. This helps the imitation look natural and increases its effectiveness.

Just as important as the speed of the retrieve is the direc-tion of the retrieve. The possibilities, from worst to best, are:

- Sit in a boat or a float tube out in the lake and cast into the shore. The retrieved fly is swimming away from shore, and all the naturals are swimming to the shore.
- Stand on the bank and cast out into the lake. This is a good position. At least the swimming fly acts realisti-cally.
- Sit out in the lake and cast parallel to the shore. The fly is not swimming in the same direction as the naturals, and this might make some fish nervous enough to refuse it, but the parallel path of the retrieve shows the

imitation to a lot more fish than either the in-to-out or the out-to-in approach.

- Stand on the shore or sit in a boat or a float tube and cast left or right at a forty-five degree angle out into the lake. This is the best direction to retrieve. The fly is moving sideways, crossing the noses of a lot of trout, and yet because the fly is progressing towards the shore, it doesn't look totally strange.

The damsel hatch occasionally offers some opportunity to the dry-fly fanatic. The nymphs crawl up on any available object and change into adults. These fresh adults, known as tenerals, have pewter gray/olive bodies, not the bright color of the active adults, and until they "harden" they are weak and clumsy. On a windy day enough of these newly emerged insects get blown back onto the water to create a dry-fly opportunity. A good imitation, such as a gray Flex-Damsel Adult, cast in front of trout cruising outside the weed line draws explosive strikes.

One of the few times I saw adult damsels trigger a rise was at Vermejo Park in New Mexico. This was at one of Gary Borger's fly fishing schools, where I was helping as an instructor. Every morning on the ponds the air over the water was a pale blue haze from the flying damsels. Trout were jumping to grab the adults. Any mating pair of insects that tumbled to the surface was immediately eaten.

I've never found a typically rocky, deep mountain lake where active adult damsels are a regular part of the trout diet. There are waters as perfect for damsel populations as those Vermejo Park ponds, but they are all rich, weed-choked waters on a valley floor. The high lakes always have some damsels, but never enough to produce massed flights of egg-laying females. The occasional adult pops up in my stomach samplings from high-mountain trout. These insects are one of those "prime opportunity" foods that fish pounce on enthusiastically whenever they see one. This instant recognition makes a Blue Flex-Damsel Adult, worked with well-spaced, feeble twitches, a good prospecting pattern.

Caddisflies

In *Strategies for Stillwater*, Dave Hughes writes about caddis larvae, "The crawling types depend on a neutral buoyancy to maintain their position in the water column if they lose their grip on a reed stem or weed bed. During periods of changing barometric pressure I've seen them get their densities screwed up, causing them to float slowly to the top when they lose their grip on vegetation. This is usually fatal; trout come along and gulp them like grapes. That's why I leave my caddis larval patterns unweighted: I can fish them right on top."

My imitations for the various stages of the caddisfly life cycle are the Cased Caddis Larva and the Floating Cased Larva, the Bead Head Deep Sparkle Pupa and the Emergent Sparkle Pupa, the Dancing Caddis for the adult on the surface, and the Diving Caddis for the egg-laying adult below the surface.

On stillwaters emerging caddisflies not only produce dependable hatches but also create some of the most challenging fishing situations. There are usually enough insects in or on the water any summer evening to interest trout. The emergers of many important stillwater species don't fly to the land. The hatching insects are vulnerable as they swim to the top, but then instead of escaping into the air, some types either swim as pupae just under the surface or run as adults on the surface to the shore. This behavior makes them accessible prey longer than many other insects.

On mountain lakes important caddis species include the often overlooked microcaddis, mainly three genera of

Hydroptilidae—the Somber Microcaddis (*Ochrotrichia* sp.), the Vari-Colored Microcaddis (*Hydroptila* sp.), and the Salt and Pepper Microcaddis (*Agraylea* sp.). My favorite hatch of these three is the Salt and Pepper Microcaddis, an incredibly abundant insect on any rich lake. Even on less productive lakes, this caddis is usually more important than simple numbers would indicate—they are an underwater egg-layer (in one experiment, Dr. Donald Denning timed a subsurface stay for *Agraylea multipunctata* at an hour and eight minutes). Every morning during July and August the water is littered with drowned insects from the previous night's activity. Match this size-22 or -24 insect with a team of two or three Gray/Green Diving Caddis wet flies dapped in the splash zone against the bank.

The Longhorn Sedge (*Oecetis* sp.), easily recognized by the long antennae sweeping over the back, is probably present on every trout lake on the continent. The emergence period covers months, starting a few weeks after ice-out on mountain lakes and continuing through the summer. The insect is most vulnerable when it is hatching. A size-12 or -14 beadhead Ginger Deep Sparkle Pupa, fished with a lifting sweep of the rod, matches the swimming insect. An Emergent Sparkle Pupa, simply greased with flotant and left sitting on the water, mimics the insect struggling half in and half out of the film. The egg-laying stage of the Longhorn is not as important as it is with other caddisflies because the female touches and hops on the surface, never landing for very long, but small trout will chase and jump for these adults. A Ginger Dancing Caddis, run across the water, attracts more fish than the natural insect—this fly actually pulls some decent-sized trout to the top.

The Limnephilidae family produces a parade of large caddisflies throughout the summer months. The Giant Rusty Sedge (*Ptilostomis ocellifera*), Early-Summer Lake Sedge (*Clistoronia magnifica*), Traveller Sedge (*Banksiola crotchi*), and Great Late-Summer Sedge (*Onocosmoecus* sp.) are all common stillwater species. The pupae and adults of these big insects create spectacular surface feeding. The trout line up behind either the swimming pupa (just under the surface) or the running adult (right on the surface) and chase them down. The wake of the fish pursuing either life stage is visible—it can be difficult to keep calmly retrieving the Emergent Sparkle Pupa or the Dancing Caddis steadily until the trout hits the fly. The imitations are big, from size 10 to size 6, and even heavy leader tippets, 3X or more, don't frighten the fish.

The beadhead version of the Deep Sparkle Pupa is perfectly designed for mimicking the swim of caddis pupa to the surface. The weight of the bead carries the fly deep quickly. With a sink-tip line, and a long, smooth pull that draws the imitation steadily to the top, the fly incites hard, tippet-smashing strikes. The takes are so savage that a piece of gum rubber tied between the butt section and the leader to cushion the hit is almost mandatory if the trout are big.

The Emergent Sparkle Pupa can be fished two ways. The obvious tactic is a steady retrieve that matches the frantic swim of the pupa just under the surface. The simpler method, and yet one of the hardest to get fly fishermen to do on lakes, is the "do nothing" approach. The Emergent Sparkle Pupa, tied with an Antron underbody and overbody, gathers air bubbles as it sits half in and half out of the surface film. It becomes a super-attractor, pulling any cruising trout in the area to it. All the angler has to do is cast the fly into the vicinity of feeding fish and let it sit there.

One of my most indispensable stillwater patterns is the Dancing Caddis. This inverted dry fly, tied with the hook point riding up, presents the correct caddisfly silhouette when it's motionless; and when it is retrieved it slides across the surface, leaving the perfect V-wake behind it. On any twitched or pulled dry fly the entire leader has to be treated with flotant so that it doesn't sink and drag the imitation under. The retrieve, to match the action of the traveling caddisfly adult, should be steady, not stop and go. To make the Dancing Caddis run smoothly on the water tuck the rod under your arm and pull in line with both hands.

The Diving Caddis can be fished singly with a retrieve, but the most effective presentation is the classic two- or three-fly dropper rig. Leave an extra tag of about six inches on the heavier piece of leader on the blood knot. Tie the dropper onto this tag end. This leader stub has to be short to reduce chances of tangling. Work the flies by lifting and dropping the rod, making the flies touch the surface in a tantalizing parody of a flying insect. This is a short-line, long-rod technique, the cast no more than twenty-five feet. Raising the long, 12-foot rod pulls the upper two wet flies out of the water. The last fly, called the anchor, stays in the water.

Mayflies

In *Mayflies: An Angler's Study of Trout Water Ephemeroptera*, in the section on *Callibaetis*, Malcolm Knopp and Robert Cormier explain how environment influences the nymphal stage. "Very early season nymphs, having come through the winter months surrounded by bottom silts and dead or decaying aquatic vegetation, are drab-colored, typical of this type of environment. Springtime, however, bringing new growth to underwater plants, prompts the inhabitants of weed beds to also take on the more vibrant colors of spring, and the *Callibaetis* nymphs are no exception. Very late season *Callibaetis* nymphs again take on the drabness of their surrounding environment. Dark olive brown nymphs are especially prevalent in habitats at lower altitudes, whereas those nymphs found at higher elevations are generally brownish olive to grayish brown."

Mayfly nymphs and emerging duns living in tributaries get delivered by the currents into a lake. These invaders can produce wonderful dry-fly fishing around the mouths of tributaries. Many times, when nothing is happening on the main lake, trout fan out where the mud deposition bar drops into deep water and hold just under the surface like risers in a slow-moving spring creek. These fish aren't cruising— they're sipping insects from the slow current.

Tricos produce fishable populations in most lakes. They seem most populous in areas that have some current. During warm weather the outlet, where there's a gravel shelf, usually produces the best hatches of male duns in the evening and female duns the following morning. The spinner falls happen during late morning. On high lakes Trico activity begins in mid-July and continues through early September, seemingly nonstop as this multibrooded mayfly pop out generations so quickly that they overlap.

The *Callibaetis*, or Speckled Dun, is also multibrooded, but there are distinct lulls between the peak emergence periods. The first hatch occurs three to four weeks after ice-out on mountain lakes; and then in midsummer the most abundant generation dominates the morning and afternoon fishing. On some lakes, usually lower elevation waters, a third brood emerges in September. Each successive group is smaller than the previous one, the dun shrinking throughout the season from a size 12 to a size 14 to a size 16. The spinner fall of egg-laying females happens right after the morning hatch—often this fills the gap between morning and afternoon activity.

Callibaetis mayflies have one quirk. The nymphs don't hatch steadily. They emerge in waves. For fifteen or twenty minutes there'll be a flush of nymphs swimming to the surface and popping out as duns. At the beginning of a wave the trout feed mainly on nymphs and emergers, but after the wave, when there are still plenty of duns riding the water but no more nymphs replenishing the supply, the fish cruise more and take adults. When the next wave begins, after a fifteen minute interval, the trout switch back to sub-surface feeding.

The best tactic is a two-fly rig, with a Shroud for the dry fly and an Olive Pheasant Tail Twist Nymph for the dropper. The Shroud, with a marabou tail that slithers just under the surface, is a dry-fly woolly worm, perfect for twitching; and every tug makes the nymph swim up towards the top.

THE USUAL RECOMMENDATION for intercepting cruising fish is a vague description on how to plot the trout's course—*note the direction the fish is moving and the distance between rises; and put your fly in the general area of the next possible rise.* This is a blind method, relying way too much on luck. There are better techniques than scatter casting to a two- or three-foot "possibility area."

The first method, Hit-the-Rise, is the best choice during a heavy hatch. When there are a lot of insects on the surface, and a fish is eating them with quick, nodding sips, it is nearly impossible to predict where a trout will feed next. There is too much competition from the naturals. In this situation keep the fly in the air, false casting, and when a trout rises immediately drop the imitation right on his nose. You don't predict the next feeding opportunity. You create the next feeding opportunity. When the fly hits the rise form the trout reflexively eats again.

The second method, Pairing-the-Hatch, doesn't exactly predict where the trout will rise next—it's more like guaranteeing where the trout will rise next. It is the best choice when larger insects, such as *Callibaetis* mayflies, are spaced on the surface. It also works on any type of stillwater fishery.

One morning, on London Lakes in Tasmania, it was so windy that it didn't seem as if sight fishing was even an option, but Laurie Matchem took me to the one place on the three lakes with calm water. He knew exactly where that would be, a wadable flat in a sheltered cove inside a ring of huge, fallen tree trunks. He also knew exactly when the local mayfly, he called it the Morning Glory, was going to start popping on the surface.

The beautiful, size-12, reddish-brown duns rode the slight ripple on the lake and large trout entered the ring of fallen trees to feed on them. The only way for me to reward Laurie for such a great job of guiding was by catching some of these fish.

"Here comes one," Laurie said. "Try to guess where he's going."

"I don't have to guess. I know exactly where he's going to go."

That is what is wonderful about Pairing-the-Hatch—the possible target area isn't measured in feet but in inches. All the angler has to do is cast accurately to catch trout. A typical success ratio for getting cruising fish to hit the fly is as high as 90 percent—versus roughly 30 percent for blind guessing.

In Pairing-the-Hatch you use your eyes in a game of connect the dots. Each mayfly sitting on the surface is a dot. You have to change your focus from wide-view to close-up. Watch the trout suck down the actual insect; and then scan the water for the next mayfly in the feeding path. Cast your imitation in the prime spot, roughly an inch ahead of the next natural, so that the approaching trout reaches—and eats—your fly first. The act of putting an imitation next to the real thing, this simple pairing, nearly guarantees that the trout will swim to that spot.

This is one of the oldest ploys in advertising—two for the price of one. Maybe the attraction is greed; or maybe, on an instinctive level, the trout calculates that even if one mayfly suddenly flies off, which they often do, there will still be one left. It doesn't matter what the reason is—the result is that Pairing-the-Hatch is much more effective than the old way of plotting direction and distance.

That morning on London Lakes spotting the large Morning Glory mayflies was easy. With Laurie leading me to one rising trout after another, the trick of putting the imitation in front of the real dun was infallible. We lost some of the big browns—up to six pounds—in the tangle of downed trees, but we netted and released many others.

SUCCESSFUL FISHING on stillwaters, even during a hatch of aquatic insects, is often a matter of wind management. A steady breeze can affect the distribution and concentration of insects on the entire lake. The mistake too many anglers make is to view wind as the enemy. It is exciting to see the water flat calm, dimpled by rises—this usually happens in the morning and again in the evening—but wind doesn't stop insects from emerging or trout from feeding on the surface.

English fly fishermen feel almost exactly opposite from American fly fishermen about the wind. They get discouraged when there isn't at least a breeze blowing; and fanatic stillwater fly fishermen are ecstatic when there is a gale kicking up whitecaps. The trout are easier to catch in broken water, not nearly as likely to spook at the splash of the line or to examine an imitation critically. But there's something else that wind does that is even more important—it concentrates food and orients fish.

During a hatch any emergers in the surface film or adults on the water are scuttled along on the wind-driven current. The top layer of water on a lake is a fluid, rolling sheet. Insects get blown away from the hatching sites; and trout often don't need to cruise to take these adults. The fish sit just under the flowing, wind-pushed current downwind from the emergence area, maybe a weed bed or a rocky shoal, and rise like trout sitting in a stream.

Once on Warren Lake, in the Big Hole drainage, the fishing was slow until Longhorn Sedges began popping in a shallow bay. The mouth of the bay formed a strange barrier—on the bay the wind was funneling right down the channel, but outside the bay on the lake the wind was blowing strongly from left to right. The two currents converged right at the mouth of the bay, concentrating the emerging pupae in the choppy water. It seemed as if every cutthroat in the lake was feeding in a ten-foot band of water. The trout hammered a matching Emergent Sparkle Pupa *if* it was allowed to drift in the proper direction with the wind flow—they mostly ignored the retrieved fly.

The wind is even more important after a hatch than it is during a hatch. All of the crippled and drowned insects have to go somewhere—and they go where the wind pushes them. The same rule applies to egg-laying insects or fallen terrestrials. All of these organisms, if they don't sink, collect either against the shore or in the wind lanes out in the lake. Those wind lanes, or scum lines, are the best places on the entire lake to find rising trout.

It is easy to spot a wind lane. When the entire lake is blown into a chop, there is a ribbon of flat water as long as a couple of hundred yards snaking down the lake. That flatness, a strange lack of ripples in spite of the wind, is caused by vertical convection currents looping from the bottom to the top of the lake. The flowing water hits the surface and rolls back down towards the bottom—and when it pulls downward it exerts enough force to flatten the chop. The roiling currents also suck any floating items into this flat wind lane (and thus the other name for it, a scum line). These areas in a lake are the major open-water feeding zones for trout. They can be fished with twitched or drifted dry flies on top or with wet flies just under the surface.

The wind pushes insects against the shore, piles them over weed beds, and squeezes them around points of land. It definitely deposits them in wind lanes, creating ribbons where fish slop like pigs at a feeding trough. The trout face into the wind-driven water, swimming slowly "up-current" if they move at all, and gather to feed in these areas when insects get concentrated by the water movement. They rise just as well—if not better—in wind-frothed water as they do in flat water. It is almost always a mistake to think that there is no dry-fly fishing, or no hatch-matching, on a choppy lake.

CHAPTER 13

September 10th — A day at Gold Lake

AFTER YEARS of fishing the high country it surprised me to blunder into a completely new phenomenon. The termites appeared on Gold Lake in Colorado; and their arrival was so strange that it was not only new to me, but totally unknown to a wide range of friends throughout the West. My backpacking trips take me regularly to the Uintas (Utah), the Sierras (California), the Cascades (Washington), and the Winds (Wyoming), with less frequent visits to the mountain regions of other states, but no one in any of these places had ever mentioned anything about termites.

Finding a bunch of free-rising, surface-cruising suckers surprised me, too, but at least there were stories of rubber-lipped fish caught on dry flies. I'd never personally known anyone who had run into a strain of selective suckers in the wild. The tale was common enough, though: "I knew someone who had a cousin whose brother's friend hooked a sucker on a dry fly once somewhere."

My seventh-grade science project was about "free-rising" suckers. The basement of my house was full of aquariums. My stepfather raised tropical fish commercially, mainly Jack Dempseys and Oscars, for pet stores. There were always extra aquariums and I put freshwater fish into them—sunfish, trout, and suckers mostly. And then I trained those fish. The only way to get suckers to respond immediately to floating pellets, to rise as soon as the food hit the surface, was to not feed them sinking food for days—and then they had to be fed floating pellets for at least three consecutive days. They had to be conditioned to search the surface for food.

Still, compared to the termites, the suckers were just a footnote on the day.

IT'S A RITUAL to fish Gold Lake in September. It's always with Jim Pruett; and it's always on my way to the Fly Tackle Dealer Show in Denver. Jim and I, and anyone else in our group, drive up to Gold Lake, which sits in a basin at 9,000 feet. We check in at the small fly shop, buy a few flies, and if we want to get out on the lake, rent canoes or float tubes.

The water in the lake looked murkier than in past years, but it wasn't stained from muddy runoff. The algae was blooming, the result of a warm summer even at high elevation. The lake wasn't dark enough to stop trout from seeing a sunken fly, but the difference in water clarity made previous experience worthless.

A size-20 Black Halo Midge Emerger had worked the previous year in September, pulling cruising rainbows to the fly. On the morning of September 10th, there were no fish near the surface to even look at the pattern. My only choices were to scout the edge, searching for trout in shallow water, or test the depths, prospecting with either a nymph or a streamer. This was an easy choice—the deep stuff is always my final option.

Our group was a good one for puzzling out a lake. Jim Pruett lived in the area and had fished Gold Lake for years. Steve Oristian had been with us the previous year, and he had figured out that the Halo Midge Emerger was the right fly. Stan Bradshaw was a guide on Montana's Missouri River, and Glenda Bradshaw was a canoe instructor and a fly fisherman. This versatile bunch was sure to try a variety of techniques and patterns. With five of us flailing away—none of us quitters or slackers—the chances were great that someone would find the trout.

The lake was small enough that we could yell back and forth to each other. We started yelling right away and the most used word was "nothing," as in catching nothing.

I paddled in my float tube back along the cliffs and bays, working the shoreline and getting a half-hearted strike for every hundred or so casts. All my tricks produced a few fish, chunky and feisty 12-inch rainbows, but this was from a lake that grows plenty of 20- to 25-inch trout. I was getting so desperate that I considered changing to a fast sinking line and a flashy streamer.

I paddled towards the lunch spot, passing Glenda, who was walking the bank, and asked, "How you doing?"

"I caught a sucker on a dry fly," she said.

This revelation ended any thought of fishing deep for big trout. Now was the time and place to pursue suckers with a dry fly—after all, this was not somebody's cousin's brother's friend hooking one on a dry fly. The miracle had happened right here; and if it happened once it could happen again. These Gold Lake suckers might be a free-rising strain.

Everyone fished hard after lunch, spreading out and covering all sections of the lake. Even after four hours of poor action, with less than a dozen trout landed, we kept flogging the water. Jim walked all the way around the lake; Steve lay out on a high rock and tried spotting trout; and Stan and Glenda, with perfect strokes, canoed back and forth. Few fish, sucker or trout, rose all afternoon.

For me this was not just another day of trout fishing. My zeal for surface-sipping suckers never faded that afternoon. After trying all the places where trout might rise, and finding neither trout nor suckers, I kept kicking around in my float tube. I broke the lake down into a grid and carefully covered every foot of the surface. That failed, not once but twice, and by 3:00 p.m. I was wandering. I had no way of telling good water from bad water. Reading a lake for suckers isn't like reading a lake for trout. The book hasn't been written yet on surface-feeding suckers. I stayed out in the middle of the lake, casting a dry fly over twenty feet of blank water.

It was no good hoping for an evening rise. The only insect that would emerge in September at this elevation was a midge; and last year had proven that a good midge hatch might bring up trout but it wasn't going to pull suckers to the surface. Even a large mayfly or caddisfly emergence probably wouldn't interest suckers. If they wanted to feed on these hatching insects, they would concentrate on the nymphs or pupae.

So what made Glenda's sucker rise? That fish had to be looking at the surface; and a sucker wouldn't look at the surface unless it had been conditioned by the daily appearance of some organism on the water for at least a few days. The food organism most likely wasn't an aquatic insect. It had to be a terrestrial insect. This was September, with a stretch of rainy nights and warm afternoons—the perfect conditions for flying ants.

In late afternoon the mountain winds reversed themselves. The ridges cooled off faster than the valleys. The heavier, cooler air started dropping, creating downslope breezes that would catch any weak-flying insects. The effect was stronger over water. The ants wouldn't be scattered randomly over the entire lake; the falling air, like an elevator shaft, would deliver its load in a certain area.

Insects started falling from the sky. They landed on me, bouncing off the float tube, and hitting the water. At first I thought they were giant ants. They were vaguely antlike. They came down so fast and hard that the lake looked like it was getting splattered by a summer cloudburst. The drop zone covered about an acre. And by sheer luck I sat right in the middle of it.

I grabbed specimens to stick in a collection bottle, but even after looking at them close up I couldn't make an identification. I'd never seen anything like these size-8 insects with dark, reddish brown bodies and gray wings. My guess—and it was only a guess—based on the resemblance to ants, was that these were termites. They didn't look like the white termites I'd seen in rotting stumps, except in body configuration, but I thought they might be a different stage of the insect.

In a few minutes trout appeared and began feeding in a sloppy frenzy. Hundreds of fish, of all sizes, cruised and gulped in the acre of water around me. I found a size-10 Brown Foam Flying Ant pattern in my terrestrial fly box and, hoping it was good enough, I started casting to trout that were feeding within five feet of the float tube. I had one fish circling me as he rose, and as he took one insect after another, I kept spinning in a circle, putting the fly in front of him. On my fourth rotation he found the imitation among the naturals—and it was a good thing because one more spin would have made me too dizzy to cast.

It took the suckers longer to get there, but they showed up at the feast. They must have come up from the bottom, at least twenty feet down. It was easy to tell the difference between the suckers and trout. The suckers rose the only way they could—lifting their heads entirely out of the water and getting their lips on top of the insect.

I caught four suckers on the dry fly and then went back to the trout. At first, with so many insects on the water, it took repeated and accurate casts to an individual fish to hook him. But no more insects fell after the heavy dump, and as the trout thinned the naturals on the water it became much easier to hook them. It became easier, too, to pick out a particular large trout and fool him.

The winds dumped so many insects on the surface that the trout and suckers glutted themselves for nearly an hour. Everyone else could see me catching fish but no one was close enough to cast to them. Jim was walking around the lake and didn't have a float tube with him; Steve had taken off his boots and waders; and Stan and Glenda had put away the canoe. They didn't come out to the acre patch of slopping fish, but they didn't expect me to come into shore either.

When the rises ended, I paddled in to the landing. I showed my insect samples to Jim and told him, "I think they're termites."

"I don't know," he said, but he added, "All the forests around this area were clear-cut twenty years ago. There are thousands of acres of rotting stumps."

AFTER RETURNING HOME I went to the University of Montana and had my sample specimens identified by an entomologist. They were male termites. Next I went to the University library and started reading. Here is my synopsis of the information:

> The usual form of the termite, commonly called a "white ant," is a pale, soft-bodied insect that cannot live in sunlight. The migratory stage of the termite is known as a "winged reproductive." Perfect environmental conditions trigger the development of these stronger fliers. The dispersal flights of termites are often scattered and knocked down by strong winds.

It took forty years of fly fishing for me to hit a termite fall, and after forty years it felt good to stumble onto something so strange. My terrestrial fly box is stocked now with a specific termite imitation—for Gold Lake, if no place else.

CHAPTER 14

Fly Selection

WINTER IS MY TIME for collecting and reading scientific studies. My basement files are full of them. But my
work on high-mountain-lake trout diets is not just paper
research. High lakes, especially during multiday camping
trips, are basically the only place I'll take trout for a meal.
It's never a lot of fish, one or two per person to cook fresh
for supper, but over the course of a summer this adds up to
a respectable sampling of stomach contents. I jot down a
numerical record of every stomach in my log book. Here's a

log entry from July 5th on Cameron Lake, a shallow lake at roughly 9,000 feet in the Madison River drainage:

> Six cutthroats—11 to 14 inches (fish caught late after-noon on a size-16 Red Foam Ant when they were cruising and rising ten to fifteen feet off the shoreline). Seventy-six distinguishable food items in these trout:

SURFACE		
adult midges—5	adult caddisflies—2	mayfly duns—2
mayfly spinners—7	emergent caddis pupae—4	emergent midge pupae—10
ants—10	beetles—8	leafhoppers—3
	moths—2	
SUBSURFACE		
midge larvae—7	caddisfly larvae—3	mayfly nymphs—2
blackfly larvae—2	stonefly nymphs—4	water boatmen—2
	miscellaneous (1 each)—3	

A lot of food forms that would be important in richer lakes, such as scuds, snails, and leeches, and even damsel-flies, are uncommon in Cameron Lake. Fifty-six of the seventy-six food items were taken on or near the surface. This equals nearly 75 percent. Actually, on Cameron the beginning of July is still early season, before the peak of the terrestrials. If anything, ants and beetles are not fairly represented in this sampling—when a fortuitous wind blows terrestrials on the water later in the summer one or the other could outnum-ber all the other food forms in the stomach count.

These personal records are more helpful to me than pro-fessional studies because, over a number of years, they tell me what trout are feeding on in *my* lakes. The records even identify seasonal variations and year-to-year changes in the standard diet available on each body of water. They also give me a general idea about what trout eat in high lakes throughout my area.

My fly selection for familiar waters is based on these stomach samplings. A broader selection of patterns for all mountain lakes is based on the scientific studies I read all winter. The foundation of any assortment has to be imitation. The key is to have at least a general representation of the most important food items in these fisheries. The available and vulnerable prey items control everything—where trout will be, when they will feed, and what they will feed on. This information in turn determines fly choice and angling tactics from top to bottom.

Flies don't weigh much, but their boxes can be bulky. As a result, my personal collection of high-country flies is actually rather lean and practical (in contrast my running water selection, which numbers in the hundreds of patterns, and edges into the impractical). I like to carry a lot of flies; a large part of my enjoyment of fly fishing is the magical promise of those little fuzzy-covered hooks, but on many mountain lakes I get along fine with a few dry flies and a few nymphs. On other waters, richer ones where the trout can get fussy, the selection has to be more comprehensive.

THE BASIC TWENTY-SIX PATTERNS FOR
STILLWATER FLY FISHING:
(11 dry flies, 3 emergers, 2 wet flies, 7 nymphs,
2 streamers, and 1 egg fly)

DRY FLIES
Terrestrials
The most important class of dry fly for mountain lakes is the terrestrial imitation. The trout, feeding on blow-ins

day after day throughout the summer, look for ants, beetles, bees, and spiders. The image of drowned fare floating awash on the surface gets imprinted in their minds.

Foam Ant
HOOK: 10–20; TMC 5230—3X fine wire
BODY: closed-cell packing foam (colored red, black, or brown with a marker)
HACKLE: rooster hackle (one turn of hackle between the two foam sections)

The big, black carpenter ants dominate the blow-in fare early in the season, but by midsummer the size-18 or -20 Red Foam Ant is my favorite variation.

Flying Ant
HOOK: 10–20; TMC 5230—3X fine wire
BODY: closed-cell packing foam tied in two sections (colored red, black, or brown with a marker)
WING: clear Antron (tied back at a 45-degree angle)

A size-10 Flying Ant doubled as a flying termite imitation on Gold Lake in Colorado. Look for ant and termite falls in late summer.

Foam Beetle
HOOK: 8–18; TMC 100—standard dry fly
BODY: peacock herl
BODY HACKLE: dyed olive grizzly (palmered and clipped flat on top and bottom)
WING: closed-cell packing foam (colored green on the bottom with a marker)

This pattern is the most important fly in my box for high lakes. There are always beetles in the stomach samplings of trout; and the fish will even break off selective feeding on other organisms to take a real beetle. The Foam Beetle pulls trout farther than the Foam Ant. It's also more visible—with the white top of the foam wing sticking up at an angle—than the ant imitation in choppy water. This is a great searching fly for general prospecting

on windy afternoons, when you know the fish are looking to the surface but rises are impossible to see.

In our fishing, the Foam Beetle proved to be a much
better stillwater pattern than a running water pattern. But
why? With Graham Marsh and Tom Poole doing the
scuba diving, we watched trout approach the Foam Beetle
in both a lake and a river. The closed-cell packing foam, a
strong attractor material because of the way it diffuses
light, brought trout rushing up to the fly in both environments. In lakes a fish settled under the Foam Beetle and
watched it for a few seconds; and then, as if simply looking at it was enough to calm doubts, it would rise to the
fly. In streams a fish would also rush up under the fly,
but as it stared at it the Foam Beetle would drift off with
the current. This is a pattern that trout like to study before
eating.

Foam Spider

HOOK: 14–16; TMC 100—standard dry fly
LEGS: deer hair tips tied in the middle (one pack
        extending out on each side)
BODY: closed-cell packing foam (colored brown with a
        marker) tied directly in front of the legs, with a
        longer section folded behind the legs, and a
        shorter section folded in front of the legs.

Spiders are another ubiquitous blow-in on lakes. The
difference with them is that they seem, on purpose, to
ride the air currents as a form of dispersal. They are
important when vertical winds are blowing through the
treetops; and as a result they seem to show up on the
water at different times than other terrestrials. This makes
a specific imitation a valuable fly.

Deer Hair Hornet

HOOK: 12–14; TMC 100—standard dry fly hook
BODY: yellow and black deer hair (alternating bands of
        spun and clipped hair) with a tapered waist
        about one-quarter the length of the hook shank
        behind the eye

WING: clear Antron (fastened at the waist of the fly)

This is as much an attractor as an imitation. It's a big bright fly, and trout will swim a long way to take a look at it. The fish often circle the pattern, apparently suspicious of something that stings, but the way to counter this aggravating behavior is to fish a tandem of a Deer Hair Hornet and a Foam Ant. The trout come for the Hornet but end up taking the Ant.

Aquatic Insects

The high-country angler needs imitations for all the major stillwater insect orders.

Dancing Caddis

HOOK: 8–12; TMC 101—ring eye, wide gap, 1X fine dry-fly hook

BODY: natural or synthetic fur (color to match the natural insect)

WING: deer hair (color to match the natural insect) tied on the underside of the hook shank

HACKLE: rooster to match the body color

I'm not sure which dry fly would be my second, "must-have" choice after the Foam Beetle, this one or the Shroud. The Dancing Caddis matches either the sedentary or the running caddisfly adult, but when it's stripped across the top it makes a great prospecting fly even when there are no real caddis on the water. It's not just for calm surfaces, either. It bounces on choppy water, but it still draws slashing strikes. It's important to grease the entire leader (and even the line tip) with flotant with any stripped or twitched fly or else the sunken nylon will pull the fly under on the retrieve.

Flex-Damsel

HOOK: small Flex Hook (roughly equivalent to a size 10)

Rear Section

TAIL: black Antron yarn (short, combed out)

BODY: high-density foam tied in at the tail, folded over
and tied down with copper wire
RIB: copper wire (binding down the foam)
BOTTOM WING: clear Antron

Front Section
TOP WING: calf tail tied at the back of the front section
BODY: Two strips of high-density foam tied in front of
the wing and folded to the eye on the top and
bottom of the shank

This imitation is tied in both gray, for the freshly
emerged adult, and blue, for the mature egg-laying adult.
It is a good fly to just toss out on the water and see what
happens. The Flex-Damsel is a prime chunk, a big morsel
for a trout to come up for from the bottom.

Improved Buzz Ball
HOOK: 10–14; TMC—standard dry fly hook
HACKLE: medium blue dun, orange, and grizzly (three
hackles palmered and trimmed with a V-notch
top and bottom)
WING: white Antron (short; extending half way back
over the body)

The "improved" refers to the white Antron wing added
to the original to make the fly more visible to the angler.
The Buzz Ball imitates a mating clump of midges. For me
it's an early or late season fly, something to toss up
against an ice edge when adult midges are spinning in a
tight mass over the water.

Antron Bivisible
HOOK: 10–22; TMC 5230—3X fine wire
REAR HACKLE: rooster (color to match the natural—mainly
gray, brown, cream, olive, black, or red; hackle
tied in by the tip and palmered to form taper)
FRONT HACKLE: clear Antron (the Antron fibers are put in a
loop of thread and spun into a hackle)

This pattern actually has three uses—for dapping with
a floss blow line, for imitating an adult midge, and for

imitating a Trico mayfly dun. It is just a good, all-around stillwater pattern.

Shroud

HOOK: 8–16; TMC 5230—3X fine wire
TAIL: red marabou
BODY: gray natural or synthetic fur (covering only the rear half of the hook shank)
HACKLE: medium blue dun (two hackles tightly wrapped; covering the front half of the hook shank)

Originally this was a running water pattern for me, but then as a result of articles in *Trout & Salmon*, the English fly fishing magazine, it became popular in the United Kingdom as a stillwater fly. My early attempts at fishing the Shroud on ponds around the Deer Lodge valley during the *Callibaetis* hatch were so wonderful that this became one of my favorite stillwater flies, too.

It's a dry-fly Woolly Worm. The marabou tail doesn't sink the fly—it rides sodden in the surface film and with every twitch it slithers through the water. As a result the Shroud is one of the greatest general searching patterns on any type of stillwater environment. The Shroud and the Pheasant Tail Twist Nymph fished with a tandem presentation are absolutely the finest combination for mastering a *Callibaetis* hatch.

Clear Wing Spinner

HOOK: 14–22; TMC 5230—3X fine wire
TAIL: two hackle fibers (split)
BODY: synthetic or natural fur (thicker at the thorax)
WING: clear Antron fibers

This is the easiest spinner imitation to see on the water because the clear Antron wings stand out brightly on the surface. With the Clear Wing Spinner either match the Trico spinner (sizes 18–22 black) or the *Callibaetis* spinner (sizes 12–16 gray).

EMERGERS

The emergent stages of the caddisfly and the midge have to be specifically imitated because of the brightness of the air inside a clear pupal sheath. General patterns fail miserably when trout are selectively feeding on the pupal stage of either insect. This is true in streams, where fish have to make a decision quickly, and even more true in lakes, where fish can perch under and study an artificial fly for as long as they want.

Bead Head Deep Sparkle Pupa

HOOK: 8–16; TMC 3761—1X long and 2X heavy nymph hook

OVERBODY: Antron yarn (pulled in a loose and sparse bubble around the fly)

UNDERBODY: Antron dubbing (touch dubbed)

WINGS: soft hackle fibers (along each side of the body)

HEAD: brass bead

This pattern is fished with a sink-tip line. The bead-head version of the Deep Sparkle Pupa, with long, steady pulls on the retrieve, rises up through the water like the natural swimming to the surface. This fly also works well with a floating line and the Hang-and-Bob technique.

Emergent Sparkle Pupa

HOOK: 8–22; TMC 100—standard dry fly hook

OVERBODY: Antron yarn (pulled in a loose and sparse bubble around the fly)

UNDERBODY: Antron dubbing (touch dubbed)

WING: deer or elk hair

HEAD: natural or synthetic fur (noodle dubbed)

This was the first fly to use Antron, the bright, multi-sided nylon that matches the air carried by the emerging insect inside the pupal sheath. Antron does more than just reflect light—it also attracts natural air bubbles. As a result the Emergent Sparkle Pupa, half in and half out of the surface film, becomes a glittering ball of silver with splotches of color. It becomes the rarest of artificials, a fly that is both an imitation and an attractor at the same time. It draws trout from a wide area, but then when they get near the Emergent Sparkle Pupa they don't hesitate in sucking it down. Whether it is fished dead, just greased with flotant and allowed to sit on the surface, or with a steady retrieve, it is the perfect imitation for the emerging caddisfly.

Halo Midge Emerger

HOOK: 16–24; TMC 900 BL—1X fine, barbless dry fly hook
BODY: Antron dubbing (touch dubbed)
HALO: small piece of closed-cell packing foam tied out either side of the shank so that it protrudes just behind the eye
SPIKE: orange deer hair tied in at the eye and slanted forward approximately 45 degrees

The main midge colors are cream, gray, brown, black, olive, and red. The fly is greased to float and fished hanging in the surface film. It has enough powerful attractor characteristics, with the Antron body and foam halo, to be effective even when the water is covered with natural insects.

WET FLIES

The egg-laying stages of the midge and the caddisfly cannot be imitated by ordinary patterns because these insects carry a cluster of air bubbles with them when they go underwater. The best material for reproducing that effect is Antron; and both the Diving Caddis and the Diving Egg-Laying Midge are tied with dubbed Antron yarn for the body and clear Antron for the wing.

Diving Egg-Laying Midge

HOOK: 16–22; TMC 9300—standard wet fly hook
BODY: Antron dubbing (touch dubbed)

WING: clear Antron (tied in a loop over the body)
HACKLE: hen hackle (one turn as a sparse collar)

My favorite tactic is to tie three of these flies together (tying the monofilament from the bend of one hook to the eye of another), cast them and let them sink a few feet, and then draw them to the surface smoothly.

Diving Caddis

HOOK: 8–20; TMC 9300—standard wet fly hook
BODY: Antron dubbing (touch dubbed)
UNDERWING: soft hackle fibers
OVERWING: clear Antron
HACKLE: rooster hackle (one turn of low quality hackle; fibers are forced back around the fly)

If no fish are rising, the first thing to look for on a lake are the wind lanes. These flat ribbons of water amidst the chop gather drowned insects and attract trout. They are the places to fish "loch-style." With a float tube or kick boat, line up along side the scum line and drift with the wind from top to bottom. Put three wet flies (and at least one of them should be the Diving Caddis) on a leader, leaving extensions off the blood knot as droppers. Lift and drop a long fly rod, making the patterns dance and touch the water.

NYMPHS

Floating Damselfly Nymph

HOOK: 8–12; TMC 5262—2X long nymph hook
FLOTATION: a cylinder of high-density foam wrapped along the hook shank
TAIL: olive marabou and clear Antron fibers (combed together)
ABDOMEN: olive fur and olive Antron dubbing (chopped, blended, and dubbed)
THORAX: olive fur and olive Antron dubbing (chopped, blended, and dubbed)
HACKLE: grouse fibers (tied as a collar and swept back)

This pattern is designed for the Yo-Yo Retrieve. The sinking, shooting-head line cuts through the weeds, stirring up insects and flushing minnows, and the floating fly swims above the weeds right through this chum slick. This is a fine searching technique when nothing much is happening; and during a heavy hatch of damsel nymphs, when the abundant naturals make it tough for trout to find an imitation, this technique is often the only chance of catching a good number of fish.

Sometimes emerging damsel nymphs swim just under the surface instead of along the bottom. This usually happens in shallow bays. The trout roll and break the surface as they take the naturals. This is the time to fish the Floating Damselfly Nymph with a floating line and a strip retrieve right on top.

Two other patterns, the Floating Emergent Sparkle Pupa and the Floating Marabou Single Egg, also are designed for the Yo-Yo Retrieve. These floating variations are simply the regular flies with a buoyant, foam underbody.

Floating Caddis Larva

HOOK: 2–6; TMC 5212—2X long and 1X fine dry-fly hook

CASE: brown and gray speckled deer hair (spun and clipped to shape)

INSECT BODY: pale yellow or pale olive natural or synthetic fur (dubbed)

HACKLE: grouse fibers (beard style)

This imitates the caddis larva that get air bubbles trapped under its case and floats to the surface. Right after ice-out, when the insects migrate from deep water into the shallows, mats of these caddis collect in the wind lanes and trout feed like pigs at a slop trough. Grease up the fly and allow it to drift dead with the wind current.

Cased Caddis Larva

HOOK: 2–10; TMC 5262—2X long and 2X heavy nymph hook

WEIGHT: lead wire (wrapped on the shank)
CASE: soft hackle feathers (wrapped and trimmed)
INSECT BODY: pale yellow or pale olive natural or synthetic fur (dubbed)
HACKLE: soft hackle fibers (beard style)
Fish this fly very slowly right over the bottom.

Rollover Scud
HOOK: 14-18; TMC 9300—standard wet fly hook
WEIGHT: strip of lead wire (tied on top of the hook shank)
BACK: eight pieces of Fluorescent Blue Stren spinning line
BODY: Antron dubbing (dubbed rough and shaggy)

The fly, unbalanced by the strip of lead along the top of the hook shank, flips over when it isn't being retrieved. This is one of the few patterns that will make trout that are "grazing" on zooplankton strike an artificial—the sudden roll of the fly triggers a reaction. It is an indispensable pattern on rich lakes with populations of real scuds. It is a valuable searching fly even on infertile lakes, where trout never saw a scud but still respond to the rolling action of the fly. Olive and orange are the best colors for the Rollover Scud.

Twist Nymph (stillwater version)
HOOK: 10-18; TMC 3761—1X heavy and 1X long
TAIL: two peacock herl tips
ABDOMEN: peacock herl and yellow Antron dubbing (twisted together in a dubbing loop)
THORAX: three or four strands of peacock herl (wrapped)
CREST: grizzly hackle and golden badger hackle (twisted together in a dubbing loop and pulled over the top of the thorax)

One of the most valuable approaches on lakes is the Do Nothing technique. Cast out your nymph and as it sinks watch the line tip for a subtle take. The stillwater version of the Twist Nymph, with the crest of hackle fibers acting as a stabilizer, settles through the water in a lifelike position. It is designed for the Do Nothing method.

A beadhead version of the Twist Nymph, with a stubby marabou tail instead of the two pieces of herl and a brass bead instead of the thorax and crest, is a great pattern for the Hang-and-Bob technique.

Pheasant Tail Twist Nymph

HOOK: 14–16; TMC 3761—1X heavy and 1X long
TAIL: two pheasant tail fibers
ABDOMEN: pheasant tail herl and orange Antron dubbing (twisted together in a dubbing loop)
WING CASE: six pheasant tail fibers (pulled over the top)
THORAX: olive Antron dubbing

This is another nymph that uses the Double Magic dubbing tying technique, a way of forming a fuzzy aura of Antron fibers around the herl body. The result is a combination of imitation, the mottled color of the pheasant tail herl providing realism, and attraction, the hint of orange Antron creating a strong visual counterpoint, that always makes a powerful fly. The Pheasant Tail Twist Nymph matches the *Callibaetis* nymph, and it can be fished over the weed tops like a resident nymph or pulled to the surface like an emerger.

Variegated Midge Larva

HOOK: 14–18; TMC 9300—standard wet fly hook
BODY: two colors of marabou fibers and one long strand of clear Antron (spun in a dubbing loop)
SPIKE: a tuft of white Antron (combed out; extending out over the eye of the hook)

The spike on the Variegated Midge Larva has nothing to do with imitation. It was added so that you can see the fly in shallow water. Try casting to individual trout and pulling the larva imitation right in front of the nose of a feeding fish. Shallow bays have too much natural food and too much empty water to throw and retrieve flies blindly and expect to catch trout. Midge larva migrate off the shallow mudflats towards deeper water after the first hard freezes of autumn.

STREAMERS

Plain Jane

HOOK: 10–14; TMC 5263—3X long streamer hook
TAIL: marabou (clipped in a short stub)
BODY: eggshell white yarn (wrapped)
WING: marabou fibers (extending to the end of the tail)
HEAD: natural gray deer hair (spun and clipped rough)

The marabou can be white for rainbows, pale green for cutthroats, yellow for brown trout, or red for brook trout. This fly is subtle enough that it doesn't make fish hesitate on the strike. It isn't big enough or flashy enough to be a threat. The Plain Jane is my favorite streamer when trout are in that pre-spawn, aggressive mood.

Bristle Leech

HOOK: 4–6; TMC 5263—3X long streamer hook
WEIGHT: strip of lead wire (tied along the top of the hook shank so that the fly rides upside down)
SPINES: two short pieces of stiff, heavy monofilament tied in about one-third of the shank back from the eye at a 75-degree angle above the shank
BODY: gray rabbit fur (still on the skin; wrapped)
WING: two whole, gray marabou feathers (tied on the bottom of the hook shank so that the fly rides upside down)

This fly can be fished like any regular leech, with a swimming retrieve that makes the marabou fibers and soft fur flow sinuously. It is also the best pattern for the Multiple Roll technique. But it is designed specifically for sand- or mud-bottomed lakes and a unique method of presentation. Like most of my flies the Bristle Leech has a trigger characteristic—unlike all my other flies the "trigger" has nothing to do with how the fly itself looks or acts.

The trigger for the Bristle Leech is what it does when it's pulled off a soft lake bottom. Let the upside-down fly settle to the sand or mud. The stiff, monofilament spines will press into the bottom. When you jerk the fly, the spines kick up a puff of silt. This is exactly what the natural leech does when it comes out of the mud and starts swimming. The little spout of dirt, whether it's caused by a real leech or a Bristle Leech, is an attention getter.

EGG FLY

Marabou Single Egg
HOOK: 16; TMC 3769—2X heavy wet-fly hook
WEIGHT: a piece of lead wire (lashed to the underside of the hook shank)
EGG PUFF: marabou (red, salmon, yellow, or pink) tied in at the bend of the hook and looped to the eye, where it is tied in just behind the hackles
BODY: pink sparkle yarn (wrapped)
HACKLE: scarlet rooster

Sometimes the only thing that will work is an egg pattern. It's fine even to cast to wild fish in an overpopulated lake; there's nothing wrong with casting to trout in a stocked lake where there is no successful natural reproduction. The Marabou Single Egg catches those fish that are too preoccupied with fighting or nest building to take any regular fly.

THESE ARE ALL my patterns. They are not the only flies that will work on stillwaters; and they are not the only flies in my box. Other favorites include Randall Kaufmann's Timberline Emerger and Ralph Cutter's Martis Midge. These are not general flies, either. They are designed for stillwaters. It doesn't matter whether you carry three patterns or three hundred patterns—the key to success will always be knowing both when and how to use each fly in the box. The key for mountain lakes is carrying flies designed for stillwaters, not a random assortment of running water patterns.

Even if you understand the reason behind a pattern's design, you may still be unable to put together the puzzle of when and how to use that fly. There's a third dimension in fly fishing—*where* you fish controls the when and how. The methods that work on infertile lakes are different from the methods that work on rich lakes for a reason.

I categorize stillwaters by the food base. In my classification it's not just the diversity of food types in any given body of water that separates one lake from another. It's the amount of food overall, paucity versus abundance, that ends up being much more important to my fly fishing strategy. In an infertile lake the trout are like wandering trashpickers for most of the day, sorting through all the waste in search of something good. In a rich lake, prey items are so abundant that when one of them hits a vulnerable stage in the life cycle, the trout move to specific areas and slop heavily on available individuals.

The main factors that hurt the productivity of high-mountain lakes are the cold water temperatures, hard-rock geology, and configuration (amount of shallow water versus amount of deep water). A fertile lake contradicts that profile in one, two, or three ways:

Configuration—

Most mountain lakes, made by man or glacier, sit in bowls or canyons and the shallows, or littoral zone, may be no more than a rim surrounding a plunging center. The shallow areas produce most of the aquatic food on a lake. The fishery blessed with expansive edges, flats, or shoals is richer than the normal high-mountain hole.

Geology—

Much of the Rocky Mountain region before uplift was the bottom of an ocean. In places the rock is soft fissured sedimentary limestones and sandstones. As water filters through layers of these rocks it combines with carbon dioxide in the closed spaces and forms carbonic acid—the acid in turn eats away at the rock, releasing nutrients into the water, and this rich, high-pH soup raises the basic productivity of any stream or lake it issues into. There is an abundance of food, including some forms (scuds and snails) that can't live in low-pH environments. Trout grow faster and larger.

Water temperature—

Sometimes the simple position of the lake makes a big difference in productivity. If it sits so that the early and late sun stays on the water, there is more photosynthesis among the basic algae at the bottom of the food chain. The water warms up faster in the spring and cools off slower in the fall. Two lakes can be within a mile of each other, on opposite sides of the mountain, and the one that gets more sunlight grows significantly bigger trout.

Springs entering the lake also create a warmer temperature zone. A tributary that dumps from one lake down into another might be warmer than normal if the water coming off the surface of the upper lake is heated by the summer sun. Or a lake just might sit in the path of prevailing winds that are more temperate than the surrounding mountain air.

RELATIVELY INFERTILE HIGH-MOUNTAIN LAKES:

The typical high-mountain lake has low primary productivity, colder than optimum water temperature for fish growth even during the summer, and a very brief growing season overall for the trout (as much as nine months spent under the ice). Surprisingly, such a lake can still grow a trophy specimen. A trout may live many years and, if the competition for food is low because of a small population, individual fish may get relatively large. Larger, at least, than the average high-mountain trout of 10 to 14 inches. It becomes a game to catch and release a couple of the best fish, maybe 18 inches or more, on a given body of water. A search for the biggest trout is a good way to make high-lake fisheries a greater challenge.

For me the worst of the high-mountain lakes are those overpopulated with 6- to 9-inch, thin-bodied, big headed runts. This sometimes happens in cutthroat lakes, but it is more of a problem in brook trout lakes. The spawning grounds can be too good—there might be miles of ideal gravel runs on which fish can deposit eggs. These are great lakes for a beginner. Those hungry trout rush anything that hits the water in their mad competition for food. These are also great lakes for taking out a limit of trout. On some western lakes the regulations specifically allow high harvests of fish.

The only way infertile waters can produce the occasional large fish is with minimal competition for food. Lakes with poor spawning sites are good places for big fish. Lakes with no spawning areas are even better. Biologists stock lakes without natural reproduction, and the plant dates and numbers are public record. If a water is stocked every eight years, it's going to have a lot of small fish at the beginning of the cycle and a few large fish at the end of the cycle.

Here are my final log notes on a nine-day trip up to the Beartooth Plateau with Bernie Samuelson and Ken Mira:

It's late July and we're still hitting lakes with ice patches. There is plenty of snow near 10,000 feet. The search is not just for ice-out waters. We have stocking records and we're hitting lakes that haven't received fish for a number of years. Rock Island Lake is planted every three years and this is the third year; Black Canyon Lake is planted every six years and this is the fourth year; Lake of the Winds is planted every eight years and this is the seventh year.

Without Rufus (goat) and Cheesecake (alpaca), we couldn't carry the float tubes and extra fishing equipment, and we need everything we have with us to catch some of these fish. As it is we're each toting 55-pound backpacks. A size-20 Halo Midge Emerger on a 7X tippet is the hot combination; and we have to use neutral density lines—the cutthroats won't put up with any wind drag. None of the lakes have a lot of trout in them and the few cutthroats that are left have long outgrown the habit of rushing for food. There's a lot of just watching the water and a lot of prospecting. At Lake of the Winds we didn't catch anything smaller than 18 inches and Ken got a 24-incher. Rock Island kicked out big fish, too, but Black Canyon was a bit disappointing, with cutts up to 15 inches tops, and it doesn't seem to have the food base to grow bigger trout even in uncrowded seclusion.

Both small and large trout cruise to find the hodge-podge assortment of terrestrials and aquatic insects scattered over the surface on these lakes. There's no pattern to the rise forms, but the fish don't miss much that looks edible. This isn't fussy feeding. The fish are hunting, and the best fly is the one that will pull trout the longest distance and still trigger the strike.

Specific hatches on these waters are seldom thick enough for trout to gorge themselves, but rising fish might begin to show a preference, if not rigid selectivity, for a particular type of insect. They rush after skittering caddis adults or sip spent mayfly egg-layers. If they become fussy over any food type, it is usually a midge pupa (and just like the natural, an imitation has to hang half in and half out of the surface film). It never hurts to match the action and conformation of a prevalent prey item.

This constant feeding is the key to finding big fish. Even the biggest trout have to be obsessed with the surface from ice-out to ice-up on infertile waters. The best fish are easy to spot in the clear lakes if the wind isn't blowing.

I get up high and use binoculars to scan a lake when the water is flat. When I see either a nice trout or a big rise form, I mark the spot. That same trout will probably be in the same area even when the breeze is kicking the surface and it's impossible to sight fish. The bigger the trout the more likely it is that he travels alone and has a set territory.

FERTILE HIGH-MOUNTAIN LAKES:

My equipment for rich valley lakes is a road show—three fly rods, three reels with extra spools for a number of lines, eight boxes of flies, two kinds of strike indicators, a wallet with four compartments for different types of hand-tied leaders, neoprene waders and fins, an inflatable kick boat for ponds, and a specially rigged aluminum boat and motor for bigger lakes. Altogether this collection weighs close to a thousand pounds—a bit much to backpack.

My equipment for regular hike-in lakes is trimmed to the ounce. The two rods in aluminum tubes are my walking sticks and aren't counted in the weight. The rest of my tackle scales at nine pounds and six ounces—and even this collection is trimmed for multiday trips if there's no beast of burden along to pack the excess.

The weight limitation is not a handicap on most high-mountain lakes. These are basic fisheries, and trout in them have limited feeding options. A floss blow line, a floating line and a sink-tip line, and two boxes of flies and a few leaders, along with a couple of rods and reels, give me everything I need to catch fish most of the time. I can match the surface foods—midges, mayflies, caddisflies, or terrestrials—or work the drop-offs just beyond the shallow rim with weighted nymphs.

The crisis happens on rich mountain lakes. I'll get snubbed by nice fish and my blood boils with the need to catch them. I want all thousand pounds of my gear. The spoiled trout in these waters feast on specific food items in particular sections of the lake, leaving the rest of the lake nearly barren. You have to put the right fly at the right depth and make it act the right way—often this requires specialized, not general, equipment.

Fertile mountain lakes, if they're isolated enough to discourage hordes of anglers, may grow enormous trout for the high country. The fish sometimes average four pounds; and in places where everything is right, there might be trout that surpass that magical ten-pound mark. The food base includes not only heavy hatches of midges, mayflies (*Tricorythodes* and *Callibaetis*), and caddisflies (*Banksiola*, *Onocosmoecus*, *Oecetis*, *Clistoronia*, and *Agrypnia*), but also major populations of damselflies and dragonflies. There are also scuds, snails, and leeches, and maybe even crawfish. And like any other mountain lake, these waters get a daily shower of terrestrials during the summer months.

RICH VALLEY LAKES:

Rich valley ponds and lakes are quite different from most high-mountain waters. They are often shallow; most mountain lakes sit in canyons and have a rim of shallows with a deep center. The bottoms in valley lakes are fertile soil; most mountain lakes have stony bottoms of hard, infertile igneous rocks such as granite. In valley lakes, aquatic weeds are abundant; most mountain lakes have little or no rooted vegetation. Valley lakes have heavy populations of crayfish, leeches, snails, scuds, and nymphs and larvae; most mountain lakes have spotty populations of aquatic insects (with the exception of midges) and few higher life forms.

Since trout have many more feeding options, and grazing grounds of extensive weed beds and mudflats, they can and sometimes do ignore insects on the surface in rich lakes. They may simply be stuffed to the point of satiation. It happens on these waters (especially with the biggest fish). This hardly ever happens on infertile, high-mountain lakes.

It's not that dry flies are ineffective on rich waters. They are often the best patterns for catching large numbers of trout—and surface techniques should be used more by still-water anglers. The problem is that rich waters are much more complex fisheries than most high-mountain lakes. Trout can find food in different areas and at different depths in these valley habitats, and unlike the opportunistic foragers of infertile waters, trout feed selectively when one food type is particularly abundant. On these waters you need a full range of equipment, tactics, and fly patterns.

In valley lakes the trout are often so wary of fish-eating birds that they won't rise when there's flat water and a bright sun. Those same fish rise freely, even during the middle of the day when the wind is blowing. The broken surface provides safety. Choppy water and any kind of hatch guarantees surface feeding on almost any lake, but on valley lakes these conditions often bring the largest trout to the top. The unsuspecting angler might never see a rise in the broken water, but for the lake specialist fishing the top when the wind is blowing becomes a matter of faith.

MATCHING FLIES AND TACTICS TO THE PRODUCTIVITY OF THE WATER:

The differences in fly selection and angling method between infertile and rich waters are controlled by two variables in trout foraging—degree of selectivity and range of feeding movement. There is so much more food in rich aquatic environments that trout feed heavily on specific organisms in relatively small areas. In infertile lakes fish feed randomly on a variety of prey items over a wide territory.

In infertile waters the fly usually doesn't have to match the natural exactly. Simple competition for food makes the fish rush faster to take a real or fake item. The main exception might be midge activity, which can be concentrated enough even in mountain lakes to make trout fussy.

In rich waters the fly often has to match the food organism exactly. The triggering characteristic, the prominent feature trout search for to identify an item, has to be slightly exaggerated so fish notice the artificial before they notice the natural, and the secondary characteristics—the ones trout look critically at when they get close—have to be exactly like those of the real organism.

Just as important as fly choice in rich waters is fly placement. In an infertile lake a trout might swim ten or fifteen feet to snatch a fly, but in a productive environment a fish might not move a foot. On some of my home ponds the trout are so spoiled that a fly has to be within inches of the fish's mouth or it won't suck it in. And usually, the slower the fly is moving—or better still not moving at all—the greater the chance trout will take it.

CHAPTER 15

*October 8th — The World's Smartest Fishing
Dog (#3); catching a 10-pound trout my way*

I DON'T want to make it sound like it's no work at all
training Chester. He may be a genius among dogdom, but
he still needs prompting. People, such as those Labrador
owners, are properly amazed when the Major tosses the six
retrieving dummies and Chester gets them one after another.
But even this trick took some coaching. The first time we
tried it Chester snatched the carrying bag and picked up the
dummies on one sweep. I had to break him of that habit.

Maybe I'm not giving myself enough credit here as a dog
trainer.

144

THE MAJOR was one of those people more comfortable talking to dogs than to other people. He and Chester would sit together on the bench after a hard morning of retrieving dummies. The Major's own two Labradors would sit on the ground while the Major talked to Chester. It seemed like Chester was becoming as much the Major's dog as mine, which bothered me even though I realized the man was walking around with a pocket full of dog biscuits.

With the early snow storms and cold snaps that shut down the high-country in late September, I was going out to the Major's place quite a bit. He was talking to me more and more, too, and coming out just to watch me fish, but one day, instead of him simply talking and me listening, we had our first real conversation. He asked a question, and there was a note of compassion in his voice instead of the usual taunt, "You're not going to get that big fish, are you?"

"I haven't given up yet," I said.

For nearly an hour we reviewed all the failed attempts of the summer and discussed all the desperate plans of the fall. We were two generals plotting battlefield maneuvers. He wasn't a seventy-five year old retired Major with a career in supplies and I wasn't a wastrel writer with nothing better to do than hang around his pond. At some moment my quest for the giant brown trout at the back end of his pond had begun to mean something to him. For me, after a summer of defeats with that fish, it was already personal.

The Major was right to wonder about my chances of catching the big trout on a small fly. It seemed completely hopeless now that even the scrub grass around the back end of the pond was going dormant and shriveling up for the winter. There was no other cover along that whole bank; and without cover cruising fish would spook at the slightest movement. I tried lying flat on my back in the grass and casting sidearm, but even that spooked the trout. The fish swam too close to the bank to tolerate any splashing from that side.

The Slough Pig, our stepladder pram, had given us our only chances at spotting and casting to the fish. After it sank, we hauled it out and arranged to have pontoons fitted on the sides. It was the only way to see a trout from far away and make a long cast, but it wasn't going to be recommissioned until next spring.

Other cruising trout, even small ones, were just as skittish as the big brown, but along all the other banks there were clumps of willows to hide behind. It was possible to see a trout coming and cast a slow-sinking nymph in his path. If the fly was right in front of his nose when he reached the spot, he would open his mouth and imperceptibly suck it in.

With no cover along the back end of the pond, I considered techniques other than spotting and casting to the trout. Now that the aquatic weeds were dying back, and patches of bottom were beginning to show, I could cast a Bristle Leech and let it settle on the mud, and then with the first twitch it would kick up silt and bring any big trout charging at it. Or I could clamp a heavy weight five feet up the leader and tie on a buoyant nymph, and then the weight would rest on the bottom and the nymph would float up clear of the weeds, just sitting there until the big trout came by. With either of these methods, I could make my cast when the fish was far away and just wait for him to swim along his usual path.

I decided finally that it would be spot-and-cast or nothing with this trout. I rejected all my other tricks and stratagems. None of those methods would be quite as exciting as actually seeing the fish open his mouth and softly suck in a

weightless, sinking fly. There were another few weeks before
the pond froze over and I'd try as often as possible in that
time to catch the brown trout.

One day the Major said to me, "If you don't get him this
year, I'll plant some trees along that bank next spring."

THE TWO TIMES when Chester clearly preferred being
with me instead of the Major was when I was fishing and
when I was driving in the pickup truck. So, one day when
the Major asked me to take a load of trash to the dump for
him, Chester jumped into the truck cab as soon as I opened
the door. We had to be back in an hour, by mid-afternoon,
when that big fish started feeding.

We wheeled into the county dump and Chester went
sniffing after the rodents and feral cats that overrun the
place. He stopped first to lift his leg on two perfect, artificial
Christmas trees that someone had tossed out. He didn't go
far, and I didn't worry about him eating any garbage or rat
poison scattered around.

I emptied trash from the back of the truck and noticed
those two Christmas trees again. They were both green,
roughly six feet tall, and made of aluminum. They were
trees; with their bases they were instant trees that could be
set up anywhere.

I loaded the two Christmas trees into the truck and,
with a dust-raising pop of the clutch, tore out of the dump
back to the Major's pond. I rolled into his yard and started
stringing my rod so fast that Chester got excited, not even
running over to the Major to beg a dog biscuit. The Major
just watched me throw the two trees over my shoulder and
leave at a trot for the back end of the pond.

I got there and spotted the big brown trout cruising his
precise path along the shoreline. I waited for him to pass by
and then, ordering Chester to creep, we both slithered on

our bellies into position. I stood the trees up, planting them firmly, and waited for the fish to come back.

I wondered what the trout would do when he saw two new trees on the bank, if he'd even notice them. I didn't cast and soon the fish swam slowly back, feeding in a lazy, grazing manner on underwater organisms. He noticed the tall, green trees, stopping but not flushing, and if trout could talk, he clearly would have gasped, "Wow."

He kept swimming slowly, but he looped in a big, half-circle away from the shore. When he came back from the other direction he looped away from the trees again. But that was all—after two detours, one going each way, he started following his old route, following the bottom contours that kept him at the same depth in his feeding route.

I kneeled, hidden behind the Christmas trees, and when the fish was within ten feet, I cast an unweighted Twist Nymph in his path. The fly was out of his feeding range by no more than a foot, the cast just a bit too long, but that was far enough off for him to pass by it. He didn't spook, however, and kept swimming and feeding.

I only cast the fly when the fish was moving right to left. For seven more passes the presentation was wrong—the fly sank too deep or not deep enough or landed too far or too close. I knew enough not to retrieve. The Twist Nymph had to be slowly dropping right in front of his nose.

On the eighth circuit, after nearly an hour of fishing, my cast dropped the Twist Nymph in the right spot. The trout opened his huge mouth, and although the leader and line tip didn't move the slightest, everything seemed perfect for the fly. I had to wait for that long second before striking, an exquisite moment of agony and exultation, ended only when I lifted the rod and felt the line go tight.

I hadn't realized that the Major had been watching the whole time from his bench. His hollering was mixed with my whoops as the big brown did something I never expected—maybe it was the shallow water that made the fish try to jump, half wallowing and half lifting into the air, but he did and the sight made me bow in abject humility to the gloriously colored brown trout. The Major, running around the pond, kept stopping to catch his breath, and I yelled over and over, "This is going to take a long time," to slow the man down.

The 5X tippet was fresh, and the dying beds of aquatic weeds left the fish nothing to tangle it on. I never felt completely certain of landing the fish. Beating any trout that large, when the pulling and straining lasted so long, meant there had to be some luck. The fly was still snugly sunk into the trout's upper lip when I landed him. In the net, on the built-in scale in the handle, the brown weighed 12 pounds 3 ounces, my biggest trout in more than twenty years, topped by only one other fish.

DURING THE WINTER the Major had a bad stroke. He never moved back to his little ranch, going straight from the hospital to a nursing home. He liked me to bring Chester to visit him. The Major couldn't speak, but he always smiled when he saw the dog. His daughter sold the pond, house, and ranch in the spring.

The new owners, out-of-staters gobbling up their bit of Montana paradise, swore they wouldn't let anybody come out and fish the pond. They didn't like dogs, smart or otherwise. They let me come out and pick up my Christmas trees.

CHAPTER 16

Ice-Up Strategies

IN 1916, in the northern Montana town of Browning, on the Blackfeet Indian Reservation, the temperature dropped one hundred degrees in twenty-four hours. This plunge, from forty-four degrees above zero to fifty-six degrees below zero, still stands as the world record. It happened so quickly that it killed not only domestic animals and humans caught outside, but also froze families to death inside their houses.

During any autumn hunters die, snowmobilers die, and fool fly fishermen caught in the high country unprepared surely die. Starting in September my pack always has extra clothing for extreme cold. It feels silly carrying an additional ten pounds of cold weather gear I probably won't use during a trip, but this emergency pack, with layers of polypropylene or wool for body, arms, and legs, along with gloves, hat, face hood, goggles, and insulated boots for a windproof layer, has saved me body parts at the least, and it has probably saved my life.

Log entry: October 2nd–6th
Big Pozega Lake (in the Clark Fork of the Columbia drainage)

I'm catching the occasional fish, trout stuffed with food, but every stomach sampling is confirming a mystery without explaining it. The trout have a choice about what they feed on in this lake. The weeds are dying back, exposing the scuds, and crustaceans should be the main food organism throughout the fall. But trout are gorging on midge larva instead.

This isn't the first time I've run into this. There's a period just before ice-up when fish concentrate on midge larvae and ignore larger, available food. Why? And why now? During the winter, when ice fishermen come up here on snowmobiles, the trout they catch will have mostly scuds in their stomachs. Why aren't the fish feeding more on midge larvae then?

The fishing was so puzzling this morning, keeping me wondering, that I didn't notice the day getting cooler. By afternoon the air was nippy but still not cold. I should have felt it. I should have folded the tent and headed out. I waited because I wanted more time on the lake. When I realized what was happening it was too late to risk the trail in the snow and dark. The sudden cold, the Siberian Express (with the emphasis on "express") hit like a bucket of ice water. I cooked a quick supper, fed the dogs, and we all crawled into the small tent. Zeb, with his bulky Rottweiler body, handled the chill better than Chester. It was snowing hard at the moment, but there was no need to worry about snow carrying into the morning. In a few hours it would be way too cold for it to snow hard—that Arctic air never carries much moisture, just cold.

In the morning, when I saw the lake that had been nearly ice-free closing up so fast that the open center was visibly shrinking, the mystery of the midge larvae was solved. A quick sampling of the muck from the back bay confirmed the answer.

By morning the air had to be far below zero, twenty or thirty degrees below at least (a straight reading—no wind chill). It was difficult for me to dress. With each layer of clothes the process got clumsier, and to button the shirts I had to warm my hands each time in the sleeping bag. Being bundled in so much material made me walk in an unnatural waddle. It was important for me to move steadily but not too fast, not wanting to build up sweat under all the clothes; and it was important to step carefully in the crisp, crunchy covering of snow, not wanting to slip and get hurt. I breathed through my nose, instead of sucking the icy air straight into the lungs. The cold was exhilarating as it hit the sinus chambers, causing the same kind of high some people get from crunching ice cubes, and it even smelled hard and brittle. The dogs kept stopping to bite the ice packed between their paw pads; and I'd have to stop and take off my gloves off and work the ice free for them and my fingers got numb. Then I'd start down the trail again, beating my hands against my legs to bring the feeling back.

Imagine cold so extreme that simply walking created its own, dangerous wind chill. The silence was thrilling. If I'd stop and listen, there was absolutely nothing to hear. No wind was shaking the tree branches; not a single creature was moving through the air or over the ground. Occasion-ally there'd be a sharp crack—it was a dead branch breaking from the weight of the previous evening's snow.

The air shone in front of my eyes with a silver shower of frozen bits of moisture, the very humidity turning to ice crystals. Everything was a new white, not just from the snow but from a coating of frost.

I had to walk six miles to the Race Track Creek campground, where my car was parked and probably wouldn't start at these temperatures. It was slow on the trail because I had to search by poking with my rod case for the numerous spring seeps that might not be frozen solid. Breaking through a skim of ice and getting my legs soaked might not be fatal, but it would cost me toes even if I could build a fire. The spring bogs I usually ignored and sloshed through were everywhere in my imagination and I couldn't remember exactly where they all were under the snow. No one should travel alone in the woods at thirty, forty, or fifty below zero—or whatever it was this day.

My car didn't start. The battery tried mightily to kick over the cold engine, but the noise of the starter finally ran down to a weak growl. I put the dogs up in the car. If I didn't make it down to the road, they'd die within a few days unless someone came, but they were slowing me down too much. It was nine miles to the main highway, and the way was a good dirt road. Most of the time this was easier than walking on the trail, but in places the snow was blown into deeper drifts in the open grasslands and they were so hard, frozen almost into ice, that they were work to break through. I kept moving slowly and steadily, staying warm enough in my cocoon of clothing, and in less than six hours I reached the main highway.

In Montana you can trust that someone is going to be driving even at sub-zero; and in Montana a local will almost always stop and pick up a stranded person. A few semi-trucks whizzed by me, creating a wind that pushed cold even through my layers of clothes. A man in a new car pulled up and let me climb into the warmth. On the dash of his car there was a gauge that gave the outside temperature. It was 31 degrees F. below zero even down here in the valley. Inside the car I began sweating in all my clothes.

We couldn't make it back up to the campground that evening to get the dogs. The temperatures dropped to forty below that night. The next morning Bernie Samuelson and Pat Iselton and I took snowmobiles, along with a jumper battery and blankets and snow shovels for the drifts, and fought through to the campground. The two dogs were curled up together in the back seat of the car. Zeb seemed fine, but Chester was shaking so bad that he couldn't stop even when we wrapped him up. The fresh, warm battery started the car. We sat there letting the engine run until it was hot enough to push warmth out the heater. On the slow ride down the dirt road the car got really warm inside. I kept the heater blowing full power, until Chester stopped shivering. As soon as he stopped shaking he dropped into a heavy sleep.

It wasn't until that moment that I felt like I'd really survived the trip.

FISHING AT FALL ice-up, with a few minor quirks, is a lot like fishing at spring ice-out, but it isn't exactly the same. The seasons are not mirror images. There is one phenomenon that occurs only in the fall. It's a late-autumn happening, exposing abundant food organisms and concentrating trout in specific areas of a lake. It makes fall absolutely the best time to be on a mountain lake, nymph fishing for cutthroats and rainbows.

THE SIMILARITIES: SPAWNING RITUALS AND ICE SHELVES

After the first few nights of hard freezes, usually sometime in early September at the 6,000-foot elevation in my area, the trout's surface feeding tapers off on the high lakes. There are still midge hatches, and these will trigger a rise, but the predictable dumping of terrestrial insects any warm afternoon by anabatic winds fades with cooler days.

Spawning

Fish that are autumn spawners—including brown trout and bull trout, but mainly brook trout in Montana high lakes—follow the same ritual as the spring spawners. They stage at the mouths of tributaries, waiting for the fall rains to swell the inflow. Some egg-laying takes place on the gravel of the alluvial fan of stronger creeks and on the gravel shelf of the outlet, and brook trout often spawn successfully over springs, but large-scale reproduction only takes place in a strong and steady flowing stream. A creek has to be large and rich enough to act as a nursery for the fry as well as a winter incubating site for the eggs. A good spawning environment isn't always a blessing on these mountain lakes. Brookies often overpopulate such waters, producing a lot of big-headed, skinny, 6- to 9-inch fish. The starved trout gang-rush any fly that hits the surface; and catch-and-release becomes an act of cruelty to the remaining residents.

At the beginning of the spawning process the trout stage at the creek mouths. They are still feeding, and with the number of fish concentrated in an area and competing for the available food, they snatch any realistic nymph pattern. As the trout become more aggressive, and feeding is replaced by fighting, they respond better to streamer flies than to insect imitations. The color of the streamer should match the color scheme of the trout—white and yellow and brown for brown trout, and white and red and green for brook trout. The "same species" color with streamers almost guarantees a slashing attack, an agonistic response, not from hunger but from territorial defense. During actual spawning trout start ignoring most flies, the only exception being an egg dead-drifted right in front of their noses. They mouth an egg instinctively.

Ice Shelves

Richard Pilatzke, talking about his Colorado high lakes, told me, "As I dragged the Woolly Bugger across the ice, a rainbow swam underneath it and every few feet bumped the ice with his nose trying to get the fly."

Once we proved with underwater observation in the spring that trout do orient to the ice shelf, it was natural to wonder about the reasons. Why do fish hold or cruise just under the surface at the lip of the ice? Is it the darkness, or the protective overhead cover? That might be part of it, but trout wouldn't congregate anywhere there wasn't a food supply.

In the last bitter days before the remaining open water freezes over, there are more vulnerable, abundant food organisms at the ice edge than anywhere else in the lake. The surface area of the lake has been greatly reduced, and both emerging and egg-laying midges, hastily producing a last brood, use the shelf to crawl up into the air or down into the water.

One day on one of the Axolotl Lakes, in the Gravelly Range in the Madison River drainage, I slid my kick boat over the ice and launched it into the water. The adult midges were a heavy peppering of specks moving on the snow. Some of them were crawling down the edge. What were they doing when they got underwater? I was curious enough to take my waterproof camera and, by shoving my arm shoulder deep into the ice bath, take a photograph of the underside of the ice.

When the pictures came back, they clearly showed adult midges clustered with air bubbles crawling upside down on the bottom of the ice. It wasn't hard, looking at these photographs, to imagine trout swimming along and plucking insects off the ice roof.

Ice doesn't form evenly over a lake. Usually the edges freeze first, forming a rim that progressively encroaches on the center basin, but springs, currents at the inlet and outlet, and prevailing winds that stir the surface keep parts of the lake open longer. As the edge moves into a tighter circle, however, trout keep orienting to it.

THE BIG DIFFERENCE: MIGRATING FOOD ORGANISMS

As a boy my winters were spent ice fishing on Crystal Lake in Connecticut. The trout weren't in the shallows. They were in eight to fifteen feet of water, usually tight to the bottom but sometimes suspended, and obviously from stomachs crammed with food organisms they were eating well at those depths.

Leeches, snails, scuds, and aquatic insects don't stay in the shallows when a lake freezes. They migrate out during the fall and migrate back in during the spring. In the spring, as soon as the ice clears, a mass movement begins and it's a major feeding opportunity for fish. The sudden vulnerability of most of the lake's food organisms explains the cruising and bottom-hunting foraging patterns of trout the first few weeks after the ice melts off.

Something else happens during this spring inward migration. Snails and case-making caddis larvae get air bubbles trapped under their exterior housing and float to the surface. On rich waters, with large populations of these two organisms, snails or caddis larvae get blown into mats on the surface and trout gorge with rolling rises on concentrations of these helpless, flush-floating food types.

For years, if anyone asked me which one was more important on lakes, the spring migration of organisms into the shallows or the fall migration of organisms out to the depths, my answer was the early season, inshore movement without a doubt. The regular autumn migration triggered heavy feeding by trout, but the whole event was much shorter—a few days instead of a few weeks—than the spring migration.

But my answer was wrong for mountain lakes.

Fall Migration

Take a quiz. List, from most to least, the bottom types in a lake that hold the most food organisms:

Sand   Weed   Gravel   Mud

In my fly fishing seminars the audience response is always the same: 1) weed, 2) gravel, 3) mud, and 4) sand. That answer is wrong. The mud flat, overwhelmingly, is the richest biotype in a lake. The open mud doesn't support a diverse community of organisms. As a matter of fact, the only insects abundant in mud on high lakes are burrowing midge larvae. But their numbers are staggering, a solid carpet of food that, for most of the midge's life cycle, is safe from the trout. These burrowers are vulnerable mainly when they migrate across the bottom and when they hatch.

Why do trout feed on midge larvae more than scuds in late fall? There are a number of possible factors. Midges are a richer source of energy than scuds, 5,280 calories per gram versus 3,880 calories per gram. The midge population is huge, much larger than the scud population even on rich lakes. Migrating midge larvae are very vulnerable, much more so than the fast-swimming scuds.

The main reason trout prefer midges might simply be their availability. Insects and crustaceans migrating from the narrow rim of shallows on most mountain lakes drop into deep water quickly. The depths are only a few yards away. The midge larvae on expansive mudflats move much slower and have much farther to travel to reach deep water.

I used to pass by, after a glance, those shallow bays with open, muck bottoms. If trout weren't up and swimming on the exposed flats, and they seldom were except early morning or late evening, I would go looking for water with current or structure, something with character.

I finally learned to really study the mudflats. For weeks before ice-up the biggest trout were in the bays all day long, but these fish were difficult to spot because they didn't cruise. They hardly swam, feeding on the midge larvae with a nodding motion, like a person eating sunflower seeds one at a time. Most trout never moved more than five feet in an hour.

CALENDAR OF FALL ACTIVITY		
Event	**Spring Spawning Species**	**Fall Spawning Species**
first string of sub-freezing nights	cruising & feeding heavily; nymphs and scuds along the shallow, shoreline shelf	cruising & feeding in the beginning; staging around spawning areas later
fall rains	cruising & feeding	spawning run begins
hard freezes; skim from the previous night; no longer melting during day	moving into shallow, mud-bottomed bays to feed on midge larvae	actual spawning in progress
ice forming, closing in the center of the lake	feeding along the ice edge on last hatch and egg-laying midge activity	right after spawning the fish are worn and lethargic, but after 1-2 weeks they begin feeding on midges (or, in the case of bull trout, on small fish) along the ice shelf

THE DISCOVERY of this late autumn fishing opportunity is a simple enough process:

1) Find trout feeding over shallow mudflats (usually bays at the upper end of the lake)
2) Catch fish stuffed with midge larvae
3) Sample the mud and count the organisms
4) Observe at bottom and watch midge larvae crawling and wiggling towards deeper water

But it was difficult to catch more than an occasional trout sucking midge larvae off the bottom. The technique, sight casting to individual fish, made the failures more frustrating. An entire fall season chasing ice-up, starting at 10,000 feet and hitting lakes lower and lower in elevation for over six weeks, gave trout on mudflats plenty of chances to ignore my flies.

I called fly shops around the Northwest and asked, "Where would I find experts at fishing midge larvae imitations in lakes?"

The same answer kept coming up, "British Columbia."

The next spring I met up with Bud Raley and Samwell Clark on Pass Lake for my lesson in fishing midge larvae imitations. We and about twenty other anglers bobbed in float tubes over a large, deep weed bed. This wasn't sight fishing the mudflats, but it was fishing with size-20 midge nymphs. The lines were sink tips, and the trick for detecting subtle takes was to watch the end of the floating portion of the line like it was a strike indicator.

Bud, in his float tube right next to me, cast, counted down a long sink, and began retrieving. "It has to be slow," he said.

His fingers didn't look like they were moving. My pulls, matching his, seemed agonizingly slow, and they couldn't be swimming the fly an inch a minute. "Like this?" I asked.

"We shouldn't have let you drink that second cup of coffee," he said. "That's way too fast."

Over the next few days, with constant reminders of "too fast," my retrieve slowed to nearly nothing—and then I started catching those Kamloops rainbows. If success with midge larvae patterns depended on minimal movement, there was no doubt why my regular techniques had failed on those mudflat trout on mountain lakes.

The next fall, on that shallow bay on Big Pozega, it was easy to see why the ultra-slow retrieve worked on midge feeders. Those trout completely ignored any fly, even one going by their noses, if it was swimming too fast. The fish noticed an imitation moving at crawl speed, and they'd even turn and follow it for a foot or so, but if it was traveling much faster than the real insect they would turn back to their regular feeding.

ALL THE PLAYING with retrieves, in this aquarium-like setting, uncovered a key to nymph fishing in stillwaters. One added movement, the retro-strip, boosted the effectiveness of any type of retrieve, and with fussy midge feeders it made the difference between catching a few trout and catching lots of trout during a day.

The retro-strip happens at the end of the draw. The normal retrieve, no matter what the speed, is a sequence of pulls and pauses—and it's the pauses that make any nymph look unnatural. The fisherman stops stripping, but the taut line makes the fly arc forward as it sinks. The imitation doesn't stop dead in the water like the real swimming organism does when it rests.

With the retro-strip the angler pulls, pulls, pulls, but then instead of doing nothing he pushes line and wiggles the rod tip to force slack line out through the rod guides. This final movement is the retro-strip—pull, pull, pull, and push. It's a reverse strip that equals the speed and distance of the last pull; and it lets the nymph stop dead for a moment. It's so enticing that the same trout that turn away from the regularly retrieved fly suck in the retro-stripped imitation softly and confidently.

The retro-strip works with any sunken pattern, even streamers, and with any style of retrieve in lakes. It creates an action that triggers an instinctive feeding response in the fish. It somehow sends trout the signal that *now* is the moment to eat this fly.

FALL SEASON—SPAWNERS OR NON-SPAWNERS?

My favorite Montana lakes for brookies include Rough Lake, in the Clark's Fork of the Yellowstone drainage at over ten thousand feet, and Moore Lake, in the St. Regis drainage at a little over five thousand feet. On Rough the ice-up will start in early September and on Moore it won't start until mid-October during a normal year. On either one of these rich waters there's a chance to catch a three-pound fish, a trophy specimen in this state. In the fall the biggest brookies are concentrated, initially cruising the shoreline and then staging at the spawning sites.

At Georgetown Lake, high elevation at seven thousand feet but a rich, drive-to lake next to a highway, Kevin Sturgess and Justin Baker mopped up on large brookies. They did it by stalking cruisers. Justin said, "We didn't start catching these fish until we stopped casting out towards the middle of the lake. Every brookie we hooked was within three feet of the shore and most of them were within a foot."

There's a progression to the insect and crustacean migration. The populations in the shallowest water begin moving first. Trout cruise at a particular depth. They may be hunting in two feet of water or twelve feet of water. These fish target areas with the greatest insect and crustacean activity. You have to find that band and keep your flies in it.

For spawners, the fall migration of insects provides the last opportunity for a feeding binge. With the beginning of the staging period, which is better fishing than the actual spawning time, eating drops to second on the list of priorities. For the males it's not the sexual urge that takes over but the fighting instinct. As the water gets cooler, the trout's need to feed subsides with it, but the rise in aggression and the willingness to smack fish imitations compensates for the lack of appetite. The biggest trout dominate the best egg-laying sites. This is why it's easy to find concentrations of the largest fish just before the spawn.

This fishing for fall-spawning trout is a trophy game—fishing in the fall for non-spawning species of trout is a technique game. Guess which one is my favorite? Probably 25 percent of my autumn trips into the high country, usually with ice-up fanatic Bernie Samuelson, are for brookies or brown trout. Seventy-five percent of my fall trips are for cut-throats, rainbows, or goldens.

In the fall, feeding trout concentrate on midges. Midge pupae can emerge from any section of the lake. Egg-laying adults concentrate at ice edges. Midge larvae migrate off the mudflats. All stages of the insect are imitated with small flies; and the techniques for matching these stages require long leaders and 6X or 7X tippets.

My rig for emergers is a two-fly system, usually with an Improved Buzz Ball or an Antron Bivisible Adult Midge matching the color and size of the adult. The Halo Midge Emerger matches the pupa. Nine inches of monofilament tied into the eye of the dry fly is the connection. Both flies are greased with flotant and fished dead or with an occasional twitch on the surface.

The egg-layer can be matched with a dry fly, but my observations of underwater ovipositing prompted a sunken imitation, the Diving Egg-Laying Midge. It's an effective pattern on all types of lakes, but it is especially deadly along ice shelves both spring and fall. The best technique is a three-fly rig, all the same fly, these imitations spread nine inches apart with monofilament going from the bend of one hook to the eye of the next one. The patterns are dragged off the ice, allowed to sink a few feet, and then swum upwards with a long, slow, steady lift of the rod.

The larvae is imitated with the Variegated Midge Larva. This fly, with it's stub of white sparkle yarn at the head, can be seen in clear water for a long way. Watching the pattern helps immensely for sight fishing the mudflats. You can pull the fly quickly to the fish and then, when it's under the trout's nose, begin the agonizingly slow, retro-strip retrieve needed for larvae feeders. This sight fishing is the only alternative to blind fishing a mudflat one inch per minute.

My autumn trips now focus mainly on midge fishing. These insects are still a mystery; and they're most important on all kinds of stillwater habitats. My last days on mountain lakes are spent searching for the last open bit of water. Almost for certain on that final day there'll be midges around to tease the trout.

BOOK LIST

Some people read books passively. When I read how-to books on fly fishing I read them aggressively, underlining sections, writing comments in the margins, and plastering pages with sticky-pad notes. I don't simply accept statements, especially ones that don't agree with my on-the-water experiences, but it would be just as silly to arbitrarily dismiss contradictory ideas. I keep notes and, with my fly-fishing friends, test all the new ideas presented by various authors.

Here is a reading list of fine books for anyone interested in high-country angling. These were the best from a large stack that I studied during the winter.

THE FIRST BOOK TO READ

I didn't read this book until Robert Berls included it on his famous list of "the best fifteen books of the last thirty years" in a 1989 issue of *Trout* magazine. This is the book a fly fisherman should read when he decides to walk away from the tracks of the hatchery truck. It's a great introduction to most of the species of trout a fly fisherman will find in high-country waters.

Native Trout of North America, by Robert H. Smith. 2d ed. Portland, Oregon: Frank Amato Publications, 1994; has splendid watercolors by Vic Erickson.

CARRY-INS

There are two books (actually tools is a better description for them) that I carry with me into the backcountry: the *Pocket Guide to Emergency First Aid* and the *Pocket Guide to Outdoor Survival*. They are part of the Cordes/LaFontaine series of tabbed, hard plastic, spiral-bound guidebooks designed for quick access to critical information.

Why do I need to carry my own books? Both of them were compiled with the help of experts who know more than I do about these subjects. Even if I *was* the expert, I'd carry these books. In my work I'm recertified every two years in emergency first aid, but in an actual emergency it helps to have an instant reference. In the years they've been in print both books have saved lives.

Pocket Guide to Emergency First Aid, with Betty Cordes. Helena, Montana: Greycliff Publishing Company, and Rigby, Idaho: Troutbek Publishing Company, 1993.

Pocket Guide to Outdoor Survival, with Stan Bradshaw. Helena, Montana: Greycliff Publishing Company, and Rigby, Idaho: Troutbek Publishing Company, 1994.

OUTDOOR PHOTOGRAPHY

For beginning photographers, this book is a fine tool to take into the field:

Pocket Guide to Outdoor Photography, with Mary Mather. Helena, Montana: Greycliff Publishing Company, and Rigby, Idaho: Troutbek Publishing Company, 1993

This next book is great, not just incredibly complete but full of creative insights, for anyone who seriously wants to take fine pictures in the outdoors:

The Backpacker's Photography Handbook, by Charles Campbell. New York: Amphoto, 1994.

PACKING WITH ANIMALS

Since there's only one animal I'm interested in packing with, I'll limit this section to one book. It's a thorough text on goat packing, but it's also an enthusiastic sales job for the animal. And it's laced with such wit as, ". . . the larger animal has the right of way. With goats it's best to get in the habit of yielding to other animals, unless of course you run into a string of pack ducks."

The Pack Goat, by John Mionczynski. Boulder, Colorado: Pruett Publishing Company,1992.

BACKPACKING

As in many sports, technology in backpacking changes rapidly. I'm a serious hiker and camper, and I like to read about all the new equipment. The only way to keep up with the latest information is through the immediacy of magazines. I wait for my copy of *Backpacker* magazine. It's available on news racks and I suggest a subscription.

The Cordes/LaFontaine *Pocket Guide to Hiking/Backpacking* gets the beginner safely onto his first trail:

Pocket Guide to Hiking/Backpacking, with Ron Cordes. Helena, Montana: Greycliff Publishing Company, and Rigby, Idaho: Troutbek Publishing Company, 1993.

Here are another two all-around references:

Everyday Wisdom: 1001 Expert Tips for Hikers, by Karen Berger. Seattle, Washington: Mountaineers Books, 1997.
Making Camp, by Steve Howe, Alan Kesselheim, Bennis Coello, and John Harlin. Seattle, Washington: Mountaineers Books, 1997.

GUIDEBOOKS

Guidebooks specifically for fly fishermen, with maps and descriptions on where to go, are popping up for every important fly fishing state. Some of these books are good, but many are so general that they're almost worthless. We're blessed to have good ones for Montana.

This acclaimed two-volume set is invaluable for the high-country angler. It covers just about every important lake in every drainage in the state. The descriptions on these waters are packed with information, and they're also fun to read.

Montana Fly Fishing Guides, by John Holt
Volume I, West of the Continental Divide. Helena, Montana: Greycliff Publishing Company, 1995.
Volume II, East of the Continental Divide. Helena, Montana: Greycliff Publishing Company, 1996.

This next guide doesn't cover the hike-in mountain lakes, but it has fine information about the important lowland reservoirs in Montana. In the descriptions it gives a lot of solid stillwater fly fishing advice for the state.

Flyfisher's Guide to Montana, by Greg Thomas. Gallatin Gateway, Montana: Wilderness Adventures Press, 1997.

You will have to judge for yourself guidebooks for your home state. You can do this by reading descriptions of waters you already know and seeing how accurate and complete the information is for those places.

FLY FISHING STILLWATERS (in general)

My basic premise is that an angler has to be a great all-around still-water fly fisherman to be a great mountain-lake fly fisherman. The mountain lakes are usually simpler environments than richer, lowland lakes, but someone who knows all the techniques for fishing stillwaters isn't going to get surprised by odd situations that pop up even on high-country waters.

The largest and finest body of literature on stillwater fly fishing comes from the United Kingdom. The anglers there are forced to be pond, loch, lake, and reservoir specialists because of limited access to running trout waters. There are magazines devoted strictly to stillwater fly fishing. The best selling angling books in the United Kingdom are about stillwater fly fishing. The English, Irish, Scotch, and Welsh fishermen themselves are the greatest stillwater practitioners in the world.

Unfortunately, very few of the United Kingdom books on stillwater fly fishing are available in this country. I've quoted from one that is for sale through fly shops and book stores:

Trout from Stillwaters, by Peter Lapsley. 2d ed. London: Unwin Hyman Limited, 1988.

Anyone visiting the United Kingdom should look for stillwater and fly pattern books by Bob Church, John Goddard, Charles Jardine, John Roberts, Steve Parton, Taff Price, T. C. Ivens, and Brian Clarke.

I've been fortunate to have many English fly-fishing friends come to Montana. Anglers including Robert Ince, John Williams, James Harris, and John Roberts have taught me the advanced tactics of United Kingdom stillwater specialists. They also send me the latest books on stillwater fly fishing. I want to write a book someday on all-around stillwater fly fishing for trout, but before I do I'll go to the United Kingdom and spend at least one summer fishing with the masters.

American literature on stillwater fly fishing is much more limited than the United Kingdom selection, but we do have some wonderful works on the subject. There are at least five general stillwater books that anyone who is going to fish the high country should read to acquire a good base of information. For the beginner to stillwater approaches there is the Pocket Guide:

Pocket Guide to Fly Fishing the Lakes, with Ron Cordes and Gary LaFontaine. Helena, Montana: Greycliff Publishing Company, 1993.

Next is a classic, one of the finest "science-based" books in all of American fly-fishing literature. It will give you a sound understanding of how trout move and feed in stillwater environments:

Lake Fishing with a Fly, by Ron Cordes and Randall Kaufmann. Portland, Oregon: Frank Amato Publications, 1984.

This book is full of great insights on every aspect of lake fishing. The chapters on stillwater strategies are the best coverage of nymph, wet fly, dry fly, and streamer techniques in any American book:

Strategies for Stillwater, by Dave Hughes. Harrisburg, Pennsylvania: Stackpole Books, 1991.

The next book while focusing on methods for catching large trout—mainly on rich, lowland reservoirs—will help anglers find the biggest fish in any kind of lake:

Fly Fishing Stillwaters for Trophy Trout, by Denny Rickards. Fort Klamath, Oregon: Stillwater Productions, 1997.

The beautiful photographs and precise explanations in this volume will help you understand the important insect populations of stillwaters:

Hatch Guide for Lakes, by Jim Schollmeyer. Portland, Oregon: Frank Amato Publications, 1995.

FLY FISHING HIGH-COUNTRY WATERS

The how-to chapters of this book, *Fly Fishing the Mountain Lakes*, focus tightly on the where, when, and how to catch trout in stillwaters. No other "high-country book" tries to examine the fishing itself in such detail, but there are four books that take a broader approach to high-country angling.

Here is a book every high-country angler should put in his library. There is no one who can squeeze more hard information into a given space than Ron Cordes—and here he does it magnificently for both fly fishing and backpacking:

Fly Fishing for Backpackers, by Ron Cordes. 2d ed. Rigby, Idaho: Troutbek Publishing Company, 1992.

Next is a volume, as fun to read as it is informative. Ralph Cutter is never afraid to venture opinions, some controversial, but he has spent enough time in the mountains hiking, camping, and fly fishing to validate his new ideas:

Sierra Trout Guide, by Ralph Cutter. Portland, Oregon: Frank Amato Publications, 1991.

In the following selection there's a wonderful chapter, among many fine ones, on orienteering, the skill needed to travel across unmarked terrain to find no-trail lakes:

Alpine Angler, by John Shewey. Portland, Oregon: Frank Amato Publications, 1995.

John Gierach writes about all high-country waters—lakes, streams, and beaver ponds—and he never misses an important point. The information on beaver ponds, probably because he loves to fish them so much, is groundbreaking work:

Fly Fishing the High Country, by John Gierach. Boulder, Colorado: Pruett Publishing Company, 1984.

This book list probably shouldn't be the last entry in this volume. I read these books before starting my summer's research, so if chronology meant anything, this would be the first chapter in *Fly Fishing the Mountain Lakes.* I love books, that's obvious, and I always get excited writing about the ones that give me pleasure.

INDEX

About the Author

In 1991 Gary LaFontaine received the Arnold Gingrich Memorial Award for lifetime achievement. Since he was in his early forties at the time, this bothered him a bit. Fortunately, since then he has continued to produce some of the most insightful and thorough writings in fly-fishing literature.

Gary LaFontaine is internationally renowned for his innovative research into aquatic entomology, fisheries behavior and fly fishing techniques. He has published widely in periodicals in both the United States and abroad. His previous books include *Challenge of the Trout*, *Cadddisflies*, *The Dry Fly: New Angles*, and *Trout Flies: Proven Patterns*. He has also joined with Ron Cordes to produce a series of pocket guides on fly fishing. He lives in Deer Lodge, Montana with his dogs Chester and Zeb.